JBS

JBS
A Biography of John Ben Snow

by

Vernon F. Snow

North Country Books, Inc.
Utica, New York

JBS: A Biography of John Ben Snow

Copyright © 1974
by
Vernon F. Snow

All Rights Reserved
No part of this book may be reproduced
in any manner without written
permission of the publisher.

SECOND EDITION

ISBN 0-925168-16-5

Library of Congress Cataloging-in-Publication Data

In Progress

Published by
North Country Books, Inc.
PUBLISHER—DISTRIBUTOR
18 Irving Place
Utica, New York 13501
315-735-4877

Table of Contents

	Preface to the Second Edition	vii
	Preface to the First Edition	ix
I.	Family and Community	1
II.	Religion and Education	13
III.	Surefire Snow	27
IV.	Sir John of Highfield Farm	43
V.	The Silent Partner	79
VI.	A Western Horseman	91
VII.	Chairman of the Board	109
VIII.	The Philanthropist	129
IX.	The Legacy	141

Preface to the Second Edition

This new edition of *JBS* has been prompted by several considerations. Ever since the first edition went out of print over seven years ago, relatives and friends have urged me to bring out a second printing or a new edition. Secondly, I have uncovered new information which deserves to be incorporated in the official biography of John Ben Snow. Lastly, it seems appropriate to appraise JBS's legacy over the past two decades. Consequently, I have added a new chapter entitled "The Legacy," which ties together several loose ends in his long life and attempts to evaluate his impact on posterity.

The inclusion of new materials has taken much longer than I anticipated when I undertook the task several years ago. The pressures of teaching, editing, and administering the various Snow philanthropic organizations have dictated priorities and consumed my energies. However, the task would have taken even longer without the assistance of numerous individuals, to whom I am most grateful. Warren Leib has provided additional data about John Ben Snow's educational experiences at the Pulaski High School and Academy. Charles Murray of Reno, Nevada, has given freely of his time and personal knowledge to enhance the coverage of JBS's role in Speidel Newspapers. Rollan Melton of Gannett West, Reno, Nevada, has supplied personal information about Gannett's friendly takeover of Speidel Newspapers. Conversations with Richard Spencer before his death verified some anecdotes in the first edition and gave new insights about JBS's role in *The Western Horseman*;

materials provided by Randy Witte, the present publisher, have rounded out the story.

The assistance of several others has enhanced this new edition. I am grateful to Esther White of Pulaski, New York, for ferreting out details about JBS from the files and memorabilia she has organized and guarded for nearly two decades, and to Ann Scanlon for reading and criticizing the revised manuscript. Lastly, I am indebted to Anne S. Young of Rochester, New York—my collaborator for over fifteen years—for typing, editorial criticism, and wise counsel.

Vernon F. Snow
Syracuse, New York
1992

Preface

"I am disappointed that the editors of *Who's Who* did not publish the racing data and other more personal and glamorous facts about Mr. Snow, but he seems well satisfied with the sketch as it is," wrote Miss Beryl Eaton about her multimillionaire employer, John Ben Snow, in 1956. "I keep promising myself that someday I'll write the story," she continued, "about this man who has done so much for so many and had such a good time doing it."

JBS aims to fulfill the best but unrealized intentions of Beryl Eaton by means of a biographical account of John Ben Snow. To that end I have incorporated in the narrative not only the "racing data" and "more personal and glamorous facts" omitted from *Who's Who*, but some information unknown to his closest friends and associates. Though John Ben Snow lived an exciting and colorful life—one filled with achievements and successes—his deep-rooted shyness and modesty precluded flights of self-seeking publicity in the national media. Moreover, his long life had three distinct and more or less equal phases, each with a different set of friends and associates. Because of this compartmentalization, compounded by the impact of distance and time, his English friends remained ignorant of his early and later life in the States, while his American friends knew little about his Pulaski youth or his career in England. This biography brings together the hitherto separated segments into a composite portrait that approximates the "real" John Ben Snow.

Fortunately, JBS saved enough memorabilia about his family and himself to make this biographical sketch possible. Thanks to the efforts of Beryl Eaton, most of the written record was carefully preserved in scrapbooks and well-organized files. The willingness of JBS's secretaries and friends to reminisce and refresh their memories enabled me to verify many facts, resolve disputed problems, and uncover additional information through interviews and written interrogatories, thus permitting me to embellish the narrative with quotations. The assistance of several educational and charitable organizations in providing me with information from their archives and files has enhanced the account and permitted insights otherwise impossible. Last, and perhaps most important, the informal conversations and tabletalks with John Ben and his circle of friends afforded me not only information but valuable insights and inspiration.

I undertook the research and writing of this biography as a labor of love. As such, I have no doubt subconsciously glossed over JBS's vices and highlighted his virtues so that he emerges as more saint than sinner. Nevertheless, I have neither deliberately distorted information nor rendered fictionalized versions of events. Rather, I have garnered as many facts as possible, selected and arranged them into meaningful patterns, and woven them into a chronological narrative. Only in the absence of concrete facts or in the presence of gaps have I resorted to inference or conjecture. Matters pertaining to motivation are always difficult for the biographer to handle, especially when the record is thin, but in the case of JBS the written evidence has been confirmed by actions more often than not.

Without the assistance and cooperation of numerous individuals on both sides of the Atlantic this biography would have suffered greatly or become an unfulfilled commitment. For factual information relating to John Ben Snow, I am indebted to Mrs. Laureda Bunker, Mr. George Cahill, Dr. Robert Smith, Mr. Richard Spencer, and Mr. and Mrs. Glen Scribner of Colorado Springs; Mrs. Blanche Prescott, Mrs. Laura Hayward, and Mr. Kenneth Erskine of London, England; Miss Mabel Jenkins of Shanklin, Isle of Wight,

England; Mrs. Alice Ruthven of Goose Green, Mr. and Mrs. Philip Nicholas, and Mr. P. Walne of Hertfordshire, England; Mr. Charles McCarthy of Dublin, Ireland; Mr. Geoffrey Head of Upper Hutt, New Zealand; Mr. H. P. Smith, Mr. Patrick Tannian, Mr. William Kramer, Dean Abraham L. Gitlow, and Mr. William F. Payne of New York City; Mrs. Robert Wart, Mrs. Frank Lebeau, and Mrs. Hugh Barclay of Pulaski, New York; Mr. Allen Malcolm of Westfield, New Jersey; Miss Geraldine Dibb and Mr. Merritt C. Speidel, Jr., of Palo Alto, California. I am especially grateful to Miss Beryl Eaton and Mrs. Dorothy Vandenberg, both of whom furnished me with helpful data and gave me encouragement; to Mr. Talbot Malcolm of Watchung, New Jersey, who provided me with materials from the files of the John Ben Snow Foundation; to Mr. Charles Murray, who generously allowed me to peruse his manuscript history of Speidel Newspapers, Inc.; and, most of all, to my uncle, Mr. Ralph Snow, who permitted me to use JBS's memorabilia and assisted me with wise counsel.

To the following friends who read portions of the manuscript I am deeply appreciative: Mrs. Laureda Bunker, Miss Beryl Eaton, Miss Mabel Jenkins, Mr. and Mrs. Allen Malcolm, Mr. and Mrs. Talbot Malcolm, Mr. Charles Murray, Mrs. Blanche Prescott, Dr. Robert Smith, Mr. Ralph Snow, Mr. Richard Spencer, Mr. Charles Stout, and Mrs. Dorothy Vandenberg. Their critical eyes and helpful comments have contributed to a more accurate and complete account of JBS's life. I am also indebted to Mr. Craig Johnson of Eugene, Oregon, friend and free-lancer, for improvements in style and diction; to Mrs. Mary Beck, for her skills and forbearance at the typewriter; and to Jean and Jonathan, for tolerating my travels and early morning retreats to the study throughout this past year.

Lincoln, Nebraska
January 21, 1974

I

Family and Community

John Ben Snow was born on 16 June 1883 in Pulaski, New York, a small village which straddles the Salmon River about forty miles north of Syracuse. The birth took place in the Snow homestead, a Victorian edifice situated on Mill Street next to the iron foundry. His parents, Benjamin and Mary Snow, were pillars of the community. His father managed the nearby Ontario Iron Works; his mother chaired the local chapter of the Women's Temperance Union. Both were natives of Pulaski.

John Snow could trace his paternal ancestry back to Elizabethan England. In fact, in mid-life he retained a genealogist to construct the Snow lineage and in 1965 commissioned the present author to research the origins and early history of the Snow descent. The following facts about the Snows were uncovered.

The musty parish register of St. Leonard's, Shoreditch, now located in the Guildhall Archives, contains this entry for the year 1599/1600:

> Nicholas Snow ye sonne of Nicholas
> Snow was baptized ye XXVth of January.

Nicholas Snow and his family lived in Hoxton, at one time a manorial estate located east of the London Wall in the southern part of Shoreditch parish.

Twenty-three years later the younger Nicholas Snow boarded the *Anne* and sailed from London to New England. Landing near Plymouth Rock in late July, he settled in the

Plymouth Plantation. He was a freeman, seemingly, for he paid taxes and shared in a land lottery. The official records of the Plymouth Plantation contain numerous references to him and his family. In 1624 he secured some land in Plymouth by virtue of a subdivision. In 1627 he married Constance Hopkins, the daughter of Stephen Hopkins, one of the founders, who had come over on the *Mayflower* in 1620 and settled in Plymouth.

Nicholas and Constance Snow had a large family—twelve children in all—and their economic situation improved over the years. In 1644 they migrated with several other families to Eastham, far out on Cape Cod, and acquired land from the Wampanoags. Subsequently Nicholas served as the first town clerk of Eastham from 1646 to 1663 and as a selectman from 1663 to 1670. He died 15 November 1676 and left an estate of £120.

Nicholas Snow's descendants were also prolific. His eldest son, John, had nine children, and his grandson, John, Jr., had eight. Most of them were given biblical names. The older sons remained in Eastham or moved to nearby Truro, while the younger ones migrated to other parts of New England or New York.

Thus Leonard Snow, a younger son of Amasa Snow of Truro, migrated westward to the Connecticut Valley. Born in 1752, he married Elizabeth Atkins on 1 July 1776, three days before the signing of the Declaration of Independence. They subsequently moved to Chicopee in western Massachusetts where their eldest son, also Leonard, was born. Information about other offspring, if indeed there were any, is lacking. Leonard, Jr. married, though his wife's name is not known, and had three surviving children: Benjamin, Sarah, and David.

Benjamin Snow was born in Chicopee on 8 February 1800. When his family later moved to Springfield, in all likelihood his father worked at the Springfield Arsenal, the area's largest employer. Benjamin himself learned the trade of a gunsmith, probably in Springfield, and subsequently worked at the arsenal at Watervliet and in a gunsmith shop in Rome, both in New York State. While in Rome he met his future bride, Lovina Warner, who lived in nearby Clinton. In 1821 Benjamin migrated farther west to Pulaski and opened a gunsmith shop in that tiny community. Four years later he married Lovina in Clinton, and the young couple settled down in a newly built house in Pulaski, overlooking the Salmon River on Mill Street. Subsequently they had four sons and one daughter: Norman, Charles, Benjamin, Jr., George, and Emily.

Benjamin Snow's gunsmith business evidently prospered, and in 1830 he and William Greenwood expanded the operation into an iron foundry. "Mr. Greenwood and myself," he wrote, "have commenced putting up a stone building, 40 by 60 and two stories high the other side of the river on Springbrook and we expect to occupy it as a furnace and triphammer shop for welding rifle barrels." The partnership, labeled the Ontario Iron Works, was successful for several years, and Benjamin constructed a large frame house on Mill Street (Maple Avenue) just west of the foundry. This original partnership was eventually dissolved, and Benjamin joined one Dodge in forming the Eagle Furnace Company. This partnership, which specialized in plows and stoves, eventually led to a third partnership with A. Fisher, also of Pulaski.

By 1845 Benjamin Snow was a respectable and prosperous citizen of Pulaski. A charter member of the Baptist Church, he served as deacon for several terms and contributed generously to the general budget and the building fund. He was selected an officer of the village and on several occasions was elected president of the Village Board. "As a Christian, a Citizen, and a Parent," one contemporary noted, "his whole life affords the strongest evidence of irreproachable character, of a kind and generous disposition." Tragedy befell the Snow family on 4 November 1848, however, when Benjamin was killed in an industrial accident. While engaged in erecting a new mill, he was struck by a heavy piece of machinery and survived only a few hours. He was interred a few days later in the cemetery north of the village.

The family never fully recovered from Benjamin's death. His widow, in her early forties, was left with five children ranging in age from seventeen to seven. There were funeral expenses and creditors to deal with as well as problems connected with the foundry partnership. Over a year passed before Benjamin's estate was settled in the Surrogate Court of Oswego. Nevertheless, Lovina held the family together for several years. She managed to retain the family homestead and kept a garden nearby for fruits and vegetables as well as a small apple orchard. She sent her children to the local academy and took them to the Baptist Church. Hers was a difficult role, but she remained in Pulaski until her death in 1866.

The two eldest sons labored in the family business and contributed to the family budget. Norman (1828-1904) succeeded his father at the foundry and became the principal wage earner. After two years he dissolved the partnership with Fisher, continuing on his own as a producer of stoves as well as gear and plow parts. In 1852 he rented a portion of the foundry building to Benjamin Dow, a millright and machinist, thus providing his mother with income for the family. Then in 1854, for reasons undisclosed, Norman migrated to Henry, Illinois, where he opened a machine shop and foundry. There he and his wife, Charlotte Warner, raised their family.

Charles, the second son (1831-1889), also worked in the family foundry for several years after his father's death. While Norman sought out business and acted as manager, Charles worked as a day laborer. The workday was long, usually twelve hours, and the environment stifling, hot, and sticky. The compensation was minimal—75 cents a day— the work tedious and risky. Nevertheless, Charles learned the founder's skills and also contributed to the family budget. His teenage diary provides both insights and information about an ironworker's life in antebellum New York.

In 1850 Charles met his future wife, Mary Kirkland of Utica, and recorded the courtship in his diary. They were married the following year and settled in Pulaski. Charles

Snow Family homestead on Maple Avenue, Pulaski, New York

Benjamin Snow Family

evidently continued to work in the foundry, still under the management of his brother Norman. Two sons were born to Charles and Mary: Gerritt in the fall of 1852, and William in February 1854. Later in that year Charles and his family moved to Ottawa, Illinois, an agricultural community southwest of Chicago, not far from Henry. There he secured employment in a local foundry and worked as a laborer for many years. Charles and Mary had eight more children, bringing their total to ten.

Meanwhile Benjamin, Jr., father of John Ben Snow, remained in Pulaski, living with his widowed mother and two younger siblings. Born in 1834, he was fourteen when his father died. He apparently received his formal education at the Pulaski Academy, although records of his attendance did not survive a disastrous fire. After his elder brothers migrated to Illinois, he commenced working in the iron foundry, initially as a day laborer.

Benjamin's younger brother, George, born in 1841, joined the Union Army in 1862 and, after some military action in the Civil War, contracted consumption and died in January 1863. He was brought home and buried next to his father in the Pulaski cemetery. Benjamin's younger sister, Emily, born in 1837, remained at home until 1858, when she married James W. Fenton, a local attorney. They had two surviving daughters, Emily and Grace.

Benjamin, Jr., now the principal wage earner, remained a bachelor until after his mother's death in 1866. On 4 September 1867 he and Mary Watson were married in the Pulaski Congregational Church. The Reverend James Douglas performed the ceremony and presented the couple with an embossed "Marriage Guide." The groom, thirty-three years old, and the bride, twenty-three, lived in the Snow family home. The following year on 28 May 1868 Mary gave birth to a son. He was named Norman Watson Snow after his uncle, who lived in LaSalle, Illinois, and his mother's family. Brought up to "fear and understand the Lord," he attended the Baptist Church, the Union School, and eventually Colgate Academy. He was fifteen years old when John

Ben was born.

When christened in June of 1883, John Benjamin Snow was given the name of his two grandfathers. *John* B. Watson, Esq., had practiced law in Pulaski for over forty years and served as postmaster from Lincoln's inauguration until his death in the fall of 1880. A respected native, he and his family, including Mary, had lived on North Jefferson Street, not far from the Snow residence on Mill Street. JBS eventually changed his middle name from *Benjamin*—the given name of his father and grandfather—to Ben because of an embarrassing sequence of events during the Second World War, a story better told in that context.

In 1883 the immediate family of JBS was small in size and advancing in years. His father was already forty-nine, his mother thirty-nine, and his only sibling fifteen. He never knew his paternal or maternal grandparents. His uncles Norman and Charles and their families lived in the midwest and rarely returned to upstate New York. Moreover, he had little association with his brother Norman, no doubt the favored firstborn, who left home in his teens to study at Colgate Academy, then moved west to Denver, where he graduated from Woodworth College and went to work in the Union Bank there. In 1890 Norman died of typhoid fever at the age of twenty-two. A respected member of the Bethany Baptist Church in Denver at the time of his death, he was buried in Pulaski amidst much grief, for he had been a young man of special promise. Thereafter the hopes of the Pulaski Snows focused on a youngster then in his seventh year.

The events of these early years—the death of his brother, the admonitions of his middle-aged parents, the omnipresence of aunts and female cousins in the extended family— made a vivid impression on the young mind of JBS. But he could also recall the pleasures of plunging into the cool waters of Black Pool, of fishing along the banks of the cascading Salmon River, of riding to Watertown and shopping at Woolworth's "Five and Ten," of picking Northern Spies from the family orchard, of playing youthful games into the late hours of a summer's night. And he dreamed of a bigger, better, and different world far beyond the boundaries of Oswego County and upstate New York.

* * *

At the time of JBS's birth about 1,575 people lived within the village of Pulaski. Most of the homes and businesses were situated north of the Salmon River on both sides of Jefferson Street, the main thoroughfare. A business directory printed in the *Pulaski Democrat* on 21 June 1883 provides details about community life. Because of the half-shire courthouse located near South Park, Pulaski was home to six lawyers, of whom two were related to the Snows: James W. Fenton and S.C. Huntington. Dr. H.W. Caldwell, one of the nine doctors residing in the village, was related to JBS's mother. These professional men as well as one dentist served not only Pulaski but a much wider geographical area to the north and east.

Three manufacturing plants provided employment for numerous residents: Tollner's Box Works, Larabee's Carriage Shop, and the Ontario Iron Works, then managed by JBS's father. The Pulaski National Bank, an opera house, and numerous commercial establishments lined both sides of Jefferson Street between North Park and South Park.

Pulaski also served as a transportation hub for businessmen and tourists. Two railroad lines cut through the village and its environs, while nearby Port Ontario provided docks and warehouses for freight and passenger ships sailing on Lake Ontario. Most northbound carriage traffic from Syracuse, Rome, and Oswego to Watertown, Sackets Harbor, and the Thousand Islands crossed the Salmon River at Pulaski. A local blacksmith shop boasted a thriving business. Three hotels accommodated business travelers and tourists. Five churches, the Masonic Temple, a volunteer fire department, and several private clubs enhanced the religious and social life of the village.

The *Pulaski Democrat*, a weekly newspaper published by

L.R. Muzzy, reveals that most villagers descended from emigrants who had come from Massachusetts, Vermont, Rhode Island, and Connecticut. The voting public favored conservative causes and Republican politicians at the polls, giving large majorities to Grant and McKinley. The newspaper supported the election of James W. Fenton, JBS's uncle, to the Surrogate Court and promoted the Prohibitionist Party which met in Syracuse in September 1883.

Each summer hundreds of tourists passed through Pulaski bound for camps on the shores of Lake Ontario and resorts in the Thousand Islands. When in the 1880s there was a real estate boom in the Thousand Islands, with many millionaires from New York City constructing mansions overlooking the St. Lawrence River, Pulaski indirectly benefited. In fact, JBS's father purchased a share in one of the resort communities.

The high point of Pulaski's social life occurred in summer during the celebration of Independence Day. The festivities of 1883 included a parade with a brass band, a bicycle race, a tug of war, a baseball game, an ice-cream social and dinner sponsored by the Baptist Church, followed by bonfires in South Park and fireworks. Pulaski was a microcosm of rural American during the Gilded Age.

In one respect, however, Pulaski differed from most other communities—its severe winter weather. JBS had vivid memories of raging snowstorms and zero temperatures, especially during the winter of 1888. From late December 1887 through mid-March 1888 Pulaski experienced the worst winter on record. By 22 January the temperature had plummeted to a record low, dropping overnight from 22 below to 34 degrees below zero. The next week a blizzard struck all of central New York. Carriage travel came to a halt. The trains stopped running. Hotels were crowded with snowbound travelers. Wells froze; many farm animals died; snowshoe sales increased daily. Storm after storm struck in that memorable year, and in Pulaski all trains ceased running because of high drifts and lack of shovelers.

Yet a month later there were signs of spring. To test their

hoses, the volunteers from the Ringgold Fire Company created a geyser over one hundred feet high at the corner of Jefferson and Lake Streets. Construction workers began stringing new telephone lines from Pulaski to outlying areas. New water pipes were laid to the Salmon River House to provide Pulaski's best hotel with running water. As these amenities of modern life progressed in his hometown, John Ben Snow began preparing for his formal education.

II

Religion and Education

John Snow's religious heritage was Protestant in general and Baptist in particular. His grandfather, having first held Bible classes in his home, became a charter member of the Pulaski Baptist Church and Society, founded on 9 June 1828 at the Courthouse. Six weeks later the Baptist Church congregation elected two deacons—Benjamin Snow, Sr., and L. V. Baker—and the following year they voted to erect a church building across the street from the Courthouse, which was completed and dedicated in 1834. In 1859 it was enlarged and in 1895 completely rebuilt along present lines.

For several generations the Snows worshiped there. Benjamin, Sr. served as deacon and superintendent of the Sunday School, while his wife Lovina presided over the Ladies Aid Society. JBS's parents, Benjamin, Jr., and Mary, though married in the Congregational Church, became loyal members of the Baptist Church after the birth of Norman and held important offices. His father was both a deacon and for many years the recording secretary. His mother directed the Ladies Aid Society and in 1888 helped found a local chapter of the Women's Christian Temperance Union. Norman remained a Baptist throughout his short life.

Young John joined the Pulaski Baptist Church in the summer of 1896. On 25 June his father recorded in the official Minute Book: "At the conclusion of the usual [prayer] exercises Mrs. Eva L. Schele related her Christian experience and John B. Snow stated that he had found peace and pleasure in being a child of God. Both of these applicants expressed an earnest desire to unite with the Church." On 6 September JBS was baptized in the Salmon River, after which he received communion and the "right hand of Christian Fellowship." This deep-rooted Baptist heritage had a lasting and profound impact on the personality and character of John Ben Snow. He was taught to love and fear God, to adhere to the Ten Commandments and the Golden Rule, to live a Christlike life. He learned these tenets in the home and subsequently from Sunday School teachers, Christian Endeavor leaders, and Pastors Milton Comfort and James Wilcox.

From his parents, in particular, he received the double-pronged ethic of religion and work. His mother was a strong-willed and moralistic woman whose words and wishes were undisputed. Her Christian ideals and Baptist standards were high, and her protective discipline was never forgotten by her son. From her JBS inherited an irrevocable legacy—a diminutive stature, severe facial features, ascetic religious values, and many prejudices. Years later he gradually came to resent and reject her austere regimen. From his father JBS acquired the Protestant work ethic. Benjamin, Jr., had worked all his adult life. Toiling at the Ontario Iron Works, whether as a day laborer or a superintendent, meant long hours and severe physical demands, especially for a small man. But he accepted his fate and adhered to the Christian faith of his fathers. He expected the same of his sole surviving son, John.

JBS remained true to the faith of his parents for many years and remembered the Baptist Church long after their deaths. To many people in Pulaski he possessed a sterling character and great promise. "Mr. Snow, one of our best young men," wrote the Reverend Mr. Wilcox in August 1901, "is a Christian worker in my church and is clean and noble." Sometime later T. B. Frary, a friend of Wilcox, characterized JBS as a "*very fine* Christian young man, very bright and a worker for God." To the editor of the *Pulaski Democrat* he was "a young man of excellent character and promise." Later in life JBS rejected his father's occupation and his mother's life-style, but throughout his life he kept his belief in God and the teachings of Jesus. He continued to believe in the Bible and the value of a Christian education long after he ceased attending church regularly. Moreover, he contributed to many Christian, notably Baptist, causes until his death in 1973.

Young John commenced his formal education at the Pulaski Union School and Academy, a public school established in 1853. He entered the elementary grades in his sixth year (1889), then proceeded to the Academy at the age of fourteen. Classes were small and the discipline was strict. The first year emphasized English expression—both oral and written—mathematics, elementary geography, drawing, and music. In the third year students encountered abstract numbers, botany, physiology, and American history: during the fourth year, orthography, world geography, and musicology; and in the fifth year, world history, poetry, and zoology. During the eighth year all students reviewed their previous work and prepared for examinations administered in January.

At the Academy JBS pursued an accelerated course of study leading to an Advanced Diploma, taking courses in advanced English, rhetoric, English literature, Latin, algebra, geometry, chemistry, Greek and Roman history, American history, and economics. Besides the normal course assignments, each student was expected to prepare for the Regents examinations by extensive reading in the classics. JBS was an above-average student, a quick learner with broad interests; he encountered no academic problems and achieved excellent grades.

He also enjoyed the confidence of his classmates, who elected him treasurer, orator, and assistant editor of the yearbook. At the commencement ceremonies in mid-June 1900, he received several honors: in addition to delivering the Senior Oration, he was named salutatorian. The yearbook entry portrayed him as a scholar:

Mr. John Snow, our youngest member, is an honor to our class. It is needless to say that he leads in all his classes, and is a source of great comfort and encouragement to his teachers. Mr. Snow has one weakness, and that is his liking for the girls. This failing of his may be well expressed in the following lines:

> I am not caught by woman's wiles,
>   Nor yet by Cupid's dart.
> I care not aught for maiden's smiles,
>   They do not reach my heart.
> I come within these classic walls
>   In search of hidden lore,
> That I may walk in wisdom's paths,
>   I ask for nothing more.

These playful words contained both irony and prophecy: JBS was very short (5′ 5″), self-conscious, and shy throughout most of his life; he also developed an aversion to women and marriage.

On the other hand, he excelled in rhetoric and elocution. His Senior Oration on "Imperialism" demonstrated his knowledge of history and world events and, for a youth of only seventeen years, represented remarkable observations and prophetic conclusions. It was an apology for American expansion in the Caribbean and Pacific Oceans which dominated public discussion in the 1890s, when McKinley and the Republican Party, sparked by the Hearst newspapers, went to war with Spain and annexed several of the Spanish possessions. (Early on JBS was a Republican, as were most Pulaski residents then and now.) Moreover, the essay revealed his admiration for the British as exemplars of progress and civilization. Realizing the importance of common ties such as language and culture, he called upon Britain and America to form a closer union and lead mankind into the golden age. Within ten years JBS would be in Britain working for an Anglo-American corporation which favored such a union.

Even though the youngest and shortest member of his class, JBS excelled in athletics. He managed the baseball

John B. Snow at age eleven

Pulaski High School Baseball Team, 1901

Hilton   Tollner   Buckley   Utley   Box   Davis   Greene
Bennett   Warner   Nye(captain)   Hardie
Pruyne   Simons   Snow

JBS as manager of high school baseball team

JBS and New York University Track team (1904)

JBS in New York City after graduation from NYU

team and played center field. During his last year at the Academy he quarterbacked the football team through an undefeated season which led to the championship of the Northern Conference. At an early age he demonstrated leadership qualities that later enabled him to succeed in the world of commerce and finance.

Initially it appeared that JBS would go to Cornell University with his close friend, Orimell Olmstead, after attaining his Advanced Diploma. However, that plan did not materialize, perhaps because of his age or parental resistance; instead he remained in Pulaski and enrolled in a postgraduate course of study at the Academy. He mastered parliamentary procedure and participated in debates and a moot court session. He also continued to play baseball with his team and assumed leadership in the Alumni Association. To better prepare himself for the world of business, toward which he professed an inclination, he perfected his writing skills, learned to type, and began to sign communications in abbreviated form, J.B.S.

Upon completing the postgraduate program, young John worked and traveled from April 1901 through January 1902. He was not interested in working at the Ontario Iron Works even though it was owned by the Olmstead family and managed by his father. He seemingly wanted to be his own boss and to prove himself in the wider world. Therefore, he first tried his luck at peddling magazine subscriptions and then turned to selling bicycles. In the latter half of 1901 he traveled to western New York, Illinois, and Missouri in connection with his bicycle sales position. In Buffalo he toured the Pan-American Exposition shortly before the assassination of President McKinley on 6 September 1901. In Ottawa and LaSalle, Illinois, he unsuccessfully sought out his uncles, Charles and Norman Snow, then proceeded to St. Louis and nearby Kirkwood, Missouri, where he visited his aunt, Mrs. Wesley Bates, and cousins. By Christmas he was back in Pulaski.

Meanwhile, his parents had applied for his entrance to Mount Hermon, the evangelical boys' school established by

Dwight L. Moody in Northfield, Massachusetts. Though JBS failed to secure admission for the fall term, after much letter writing he entered in January 1902 with high hopes of preparing himself for a career in business. His tenure there, however, proved to be short and bitter. He remained for only one term and thereafter reacted negatively to the school's restrictive style of life. Nonetheless his academic performance remained above reproach. He passed all his courses, including Bible and Latin, and attained "excellent" ratings in grammar, history, geography, and deportment. After leaving Northfield for home, he stopped to visit his favorite cousin, Anna Caldwell, who lived in Hagaman Mills, a small village near Amsterdam, New York.

In the summer of 1902, at the age of nineteen, JBS declared his independence and struck out on his own. About the same time, in a symbolic gesture, he began to smoke cigars—a pleasure that he continued to enjoy for over seventy years. Similarly, upon leaving Pulaski, he vowed never again to eat any bruised apples, as he had been compelled to do because of a family regulation. His secretary, Beryl Eaton, recalls:

> On the train to New York City he bought an apple, a beautiful Northern Spy, and he thought about it and the poor apples he'd had through the years. Right then and there he made a decision which he believes changed his whole life—the decision to work hard and have only the better things in life—no more imperfect apples or second best of anything.

For a person with JBS's abilities and ambitions, New York City served as a gigantic magnet. Here was the hub of American finance and commerce. Here the giants of American capitalism—the Vanderbilts, the Rockefellers, the Woolworths—lived and conducted their businesses. Here a village boy from upstate could, in the style of Horatio Alger's heroes, make good by working hard, living a clean life, and meeting the right people. Here also he could obtain an advanced business-oriented education in the commercial sciences.

To these ends JBS matriculated in New York University's recently founded School of Commerce and enrolled in a course of study leading to a BS degree. The founder and first dean of the school, Charles Waldo Haskins, was the senior member of Haskins and Sells, a Wall Street accounting firm. All the faculty members, experienced and well-established financial experts and accountants, believed that business should be both scientific in method and professional in purpose. They held their classes in the late afternoons and evenings at the Washington Square campus.

Here, after floundering for over a year, JBS found himself. In contrast to his earlier education, his studies at NYU related primarily to the world of business, and he acquired knowledge and skills related to his aspiration of becoming a super-salesman or big businessman. He crowded twenty-four courses, each demanding anywhere from thirty to sixty hours of class a semester, into an accelerated program. Although not at the head of the class of 1904, he achieved an enviable record and was elected class historian in 1903 and president in 1904. For some undisclosed reason he was nicknamed "Doc" by his classmates.

Doc Snow took some time from his busy schedule to take part in extracurricular activities. Besides editing the student newspaper and the yearbook, he brought recognition to NYU and secured a letter by winning several events at track meets held on the University Heights campus in the Bronx. Exceedingly self-disciplined, he ran five miles each day and participated in a body-building program. He also retained his reputation on the baseball diamond.

In 1902 and 1903 he supplemented his work in the School of Commerce with studies in the College of Arts and Science taken at the University Heights campus. As a special student, he enrolled in courses in political science and Spanish. His exposure to Iberian culture in the latter course perhaps accounted for his subsequent interest in Spanish-style architecture and furniture. During these years JBS became a joiner, a gregarious belonger. As editor of *The University*

Triangle and as class president, he became the focal point of campus news and class gossip. He belonged both to the 12 P.M. Club which met regularly for lunch and to Alpha Kappa Psi fraternity, participating in various activities of the NYU chapter.

Instead of living with his fraternity brothers in the chapter house, JBS roomed in the home of his cousin, Emily Hoyt, at 17 East 95th Street and, through arrangements made by his mother, took some of his meals there. Emily, the elder daughter of his Aunt Emily Fenton, was married to James T. Hoyt of Baltimore, a professor at Barnard College. Their family circle included two daughters, Jessie, three years older than JBS, and Sarah, two years younger. Although he reacted negatively to the predominance of women, the arrangment gave him a home-away-from-home. That he appreciated the hospitality and felt indebted to the Hoyts was apparent decades later when he became the benefactor of both Jessie and Sarah, neither of whom married.

How JBS managed to pay for his education remains a mystery. He undoubtedly kept costs down by living with his cousins, and he may have received some financial assistance from his parents. He appears to have worked part-time in a Wall Street brokerage firm and for a while assisted the president of the American Banker's Association, A. B. Sprague. At the age of twenty-one, shortly after receiving his BS degree from NYU, young Snow took a position with Haskins and Sells, the accounting firm headed by the dean of the School of Commerce. He started at the bottom, as a junior accountant, and commenced to learn the intricacies of finance. He also came to know Wall Street as an insider and acquired firsthand knowledge of the stock market.

At about this time or earlier, JBS began to attend the Fifth Avenue Baptist Church, otherwise known as Rockefeller's Church, in mid-Manhattan. He also joined the Young Men's Bible Class and participated in the various social events held in its clubrooms at 11 West 45th Street. Through these affiliations he became acquainted with the

Rockefeller family, even with John D. Rockefeller, Sr., the grand patriarch of the family, and spent many Sunday evenings in the Rockefeller mansion on West 54th Street. While he received fatherly advice from JDR, Sr., he apparently had closer ties with JDR, Jr., and his family. Through these associations he encountered not high society but preachers, teachers, business leaders, and temperance workers, all of whom enjoyed the Rockefeller largesse.

The Rockefeller empire, then reputed to be worth nearly $100,000,000, was expanding throughout the United States and the world. JDR, Jr., a young and dynamic business executive who founded and sponsored the Young Men's Bible Class that JBS attended, was assuming a larger leadership role in that empire, while his father was devoting more and more time to investing in philanthropic ventures. He had richly endowed the University of Chicago, established the Rockefeller Institute for Medical Research, and would soon launch the Rockefeller Foundation.

The Rockefeller creed left a firm imprint on the budding businessman from upstate New York. The study of the Bible was good for businessmen, so believed JDR, Jr., for it could "upbuild the man, spiritually, mentally, socially, physically." The Rockefellers became heroes to JBS; they were exemplars of the Living Word and worthy of imitation. They were the type of stewards that he would one day become — after he made his first million.

III

Surefire Snow

In 1906 JBS resigned his position at Haskins and Sells in order to work for F. W. Woolworth. Beginning at the bottom, as did all would-be Woolworth executives, he was at first a stock boy in the basement of Manhattan's Sixth Avenue Five and Ten but rapidly became the favored employee of Fred M. Woolworth, the store manager, who was Frank W. Woolworth's cousin and successor.

Prior to joining Woolworth's, JBS had thought of striking out on his own and becoming a manufacturer of celluloid collars, but, before doing so, wisely sought the advice of Harry Moody. A former resident of Pulaski and a business associate of F. W. Woolworth, Moody was at that time a director in the company. He pointed out the unlimited opportunities in mass merchandising and suggested that young Snow give Woolworth's a try. Acting on Moody's advice, JBS also talked with Harold Hall, manager of the store at Eighth Avenue and 38th Street in New York. While there, he happened to meet Fred Woolworth in what proved to be a fortuitous encounter.

JBS was in fact declining Harold Hall's job offer when Fred Woolworth came from the rear of the store, introduced himself, and added his advice to that of Hall. Except for the fact that F. W. Woolworth did not particularly care for college graduates, Snow had the many other qualifications Woolworth desired in his store managers' employees. He liked men from upstate New York, for he too came from the shores of Lake Ontario. Moreover, young Snow appeared to have the characteristics of honesty and willingness to work, and he couldn't conceal his burning desire to become financially independent.

After some initial hesitation JBS took the job on a trial basis but, at his own insistence, without pay. Within a few weeks, however, he found the position in the expanding Woolworth empire to his liking. Early on he established himself as a hard-working, no-nonsense merchandiser. He had been an independent salesman for one year and had studied marketing and finance at NYU's School of Commerce. Now, given the opportunity to merchandise the masses through chain stores, he took to it with unbridled enthusiasm.

JBS did not excel in selling; instead his forte was buying. Woolworth's merchandising shunned the hard sell and emphasized the subtleties associated with novelties and varieties, with fads, displays, and newspaper advertising. Thus the items sold themselves. Woolworth's management relied upon low-paid clerks to take in the nickels and dimes, to be sure, but the clerk did little to sell the novelty. In this system of mass merchandising, the buyer was really the seller. JBS proved to be a superb buyer.

When JBS joined Woolworth's, the company was fast expanding into a national enterprise and, like the A&P chain store operation, was establishing stores in the major population centers. Founder Frank W. Woolworth, after an initial failure in Utica, achieved overwhelming success in Pennsylvania, first in Lancaster, then in Scranton and Harrisburg, and then in Newark and Paterson, New Jersey, Holyoke and Boston, Massachusetts, and Washington, DC., all before attempting to merchandise in New York City. Even then he situated his first store in Brooklyn near Flatbush Avenue. Finally in 1896 F.W. Woolworth opened his first Manhattan store on Sixth Avenue near 17th Street in the heart of the retail district. For the building he paid the unheard-of rent of $20,000 a year. This pioneer effort soon became *the* New York store and, as such, the training center for prospective managers within Woolworth's commercial empire. Here, under the supervision of Fred Woolworth, JBS began work in 1906.

The following year, at age twenty-four, JBS transferred to Port Jervis, New York, to open a new Five and Ten. There, in his first real management position, he proved his worth to the Woolworth dynasty. Located about fifty-five miles northwest of New York City along the banks of the Delaware River, Port Jervis was a bustling transportation hub in the first decade of the twentieth century. JBS established a rapport with the community leaders, especially with Merritt C. Speidel, the editor of the *Port Jervis Daily Union*, the town's only newspaper. The store had a choice location in the middle of the downtown area. The newspaper provided the principal advertising medium. The customers supplied the nickels and dimes as JBS accumulated and deposited dollars in the bank and demonstrated his merchandising skill. The store is still operating at the same location.

While in Port Jervis JBS became deeply involved in the First Baptist Church as a trustee of the corporation and a leader of a young men's Bible class. News about the class reached the Fifth Avenue Baptist Church in New York and John D. Rockefeller, Jr. Impressed by the endeavor, he sent a congratulatory letter which JBS always cherished:

> Dear Mr. Snow:
>
> I have recently learned from Mr. Troxell that you are leader of a Bible Class in Port Jervis with a membership of sixty-five and an average attendance of thirty-five. This is truly good news and I am glad to send my hearty congratulations to you and the class upon the good work which you are doing together.
>
> If in any sense the work of the Bible Class of the Fifth Avenue Baptist Church may be regarded as responsible for the class which you have established, we can truly feel that good is being accomplished.
>
> I can think of no better or more satisfactory way of indicating your appreciation of the helpfulness received from our Men's Class than such a practical application to the benefits which you are making in behalf of other

young men.

Be assured of my deep interest in your work, and of my best wishes for its continued success.

Very sincerely,
John D. Rockefeller, Jr.

JBS also served on the Port Jervis Lecture and Entertainment Board and joined the Deerpark Club, in all likelihood through the sponsorship of his friend Merritt Speidel.

Within a year JBS returned to New York City at the request of F. W. himself to manage a new store located at 47th Street and Eighth Avenue. Here in mid-Manhattan he had the opportunity to compete with the giant retailers of the city. Before long he secured a management contract guaranteeing him a percentage of the profit, which he signed on 10 February 1908 in the presence of president F. W. Woolworth and Hubert T. Parsons, then secretary-treasurer. JBS agreed to manage the store in return for the sum of $10 a week plus 25 percent of the net profits.

A year later JBS received ill tidings from Pulaski, for in March 1909, after suffering at home for several weeks, his father went to Good Shepherd Hospital in Syracuse to undergo surgery. The operation was a success and Benjamin Snow rallied briefly but in mid-April took a turn for the worse. Responding to his mother's call, JBS rushed to Syracuse and was at the bedside when his father died on 25 April at the age of seventy-five. JBS returned to Pulaski with his mother for the funeral service held in the Baptist Church and conducted by the Snow family's old friend, the Reverend James Wilcox. His father's Masonic brothers bore the casket to the grave.

Shortly after returning to New York, JBS received the most challenging opportunity of his life. Having established variety stores throughout the United States, Woolworth's now decided to invade the mass markets of the British Isles, which F. W. had observed when traveling in England several years before. In the summer of 1909 a team of key executives, including F. W. Woolworth, Fred Woolworth, and future president Byron Miller, searched England for strategic store locations and a national headquarters. This advance party wasted no time, for by summer's end all was ready for the Yankee invasion. They formed an English company, F. W. Woolworth & Co. Limited, with capital of over £50,000, set up central buying offices in London, and signed a lease for the pioneer store in Liverpool. They also decided that the managerial staff would be composed of energetic Englishmen and enterprising Americans.

While some members of this party remained in England to prepare for the circus-like opening of the Liverpool store on Guy Fawkes Day 1909, the Woolworths returned to the States in search of young and ambitious merchandisers. Among those they turned to was the promising Pulaskian who had proved himself in both Port Jervis and New York City. JBS could not resist this challenge. Here was keen competition. Here was potential success and a rare opportunity to see the world, live in the land of his forebears, and make good all at the same time.

JBS embarked for Liverpool during the third week of January 1910 on the fateful Cunard Line ship, the *Lusitania*. "Friends from Port Jervis, Albany, New York City, and other points were at the pier at West 14th Street, when the big ocean liner left to bid Mr. Snow bon voyage and Godspeed on his new European enterprise," so reported the *Port Jervis Daily Union*. Foremost among the friends was editor Merritt Speidel, who published a news account of the event.

John Ben arrived in Liverpool on 2 February and took up residence at 25 Church Street. His first assignment was to assist in opening several new Woolworth stores in northern England, especially in Lancashire and Yorkshire. At that time F. W. Woolworth & Co. Ltd. consisted of the pioneer store in Liverpool and offices in London. Three decades later, when JBS retired and returned to America, there were 766 stores organized into three regional districts with thousands of employees and millions of British customers. He contributed greatly to the success of this enterprise; in fact, he made much of it possible.

For nearly four years JBS headed the northern district office, then located in Liverpool, and worked closely with both American and English executives. His superiors were Fred Woolworth and Byron Miller, both of whom resided and worked in London, and William L. Stephenson, a bright and enterprising Englishman handpicked by F. W. himself to manage stores in the Liverpool area. JBS worked closely with Stephenson; together they put into operation Woolworth's master merchandising plan.

Using tactics well-tested in the States, the Snow-Stephenson team increased sales in Liverpool and opened up new stores as rapidly as possible. They selected sites for the "Threepenny and Sixpenny" stores on the busiest thoroughfares in the most densely populated areas. They introduced brightly colored storefronts (usually red and gold), sensational window displays, marked prices, and offered cut-rate "comers" to attract potential customers.

JBS organized the opening day fanfare for Woolworth's second store in Preston, for the third on London Road in Liverpool, for the fourth in Manchester, and for the fifth in Leeds—all in the northern region. He apparently relished these grand openings and made them his specialty. Each featured something new, something extraordinary, something sensational—fireworks displays, band concerts, giveaways—to attract attention and break down British resistance to the Yankee style of mass merchandising.

The opening of the second store in Liverpool attracted national attention. Thousands of curiosity-seekers and customers crowded London Road hours before the opening. Then a riot broke out when a mob of bargain-hungry women broke down the doors, pushed the counters around the floor, and picked over the items. Some salesladies fainted, whereupon the management called in the local police to restore order. Though this free publicity meant money in the till, at the next opening the Snow-Stephenson team used barriers and ropes to hold back overeager bargain-hunters. The success resulting from these circus-like openings—in terms of both pounds sterling and pub-

Christmas card showing JBS's Woolworth Store in Liverpool, England (1909)

JBS as Woolworth executive (ca. 1911)

B. D. MILLER,
Director, English Company ; President F. W. Woolworth Co., N.Y.

C. H. HUBBARD,
Assistant Managing Director.

J. B. SNOW
Director, and Superintendent of Buying.

F. W. WOOLWORTH  & CO., LIMITED.

Woolworth's English management team (1934)

Woolworth House in London, England (1930)

licity—must be attributed to John Ben Snow. When he zeroed in on an opening, he took aim, called his shots carefully, fired away—and was always on target. He soon won not only the admiration of his cohorts but an appropriate nickname: "Surefire Snow."

For these and other personal triumphs, Surefire Snow received plaudits from Woolworth executives on both sides of the Atlantic which soon proved profitable in terms of advancement, status, and salary. In 1913 he was promoted to buyer, an upper management position, and soon thereafter became a director of the British corporation. These promotions mandated a move to London, the corporate headquarters, where he took up residence at Clarendon Court, a luxurious Victorian building located in Maida Vale. His Woolworth office was situated on Oxford Street, where he associated more closely with the top executives— Fred Woolworth, Byron Miller, William Stephenson, and Charles Hubbard. A bachelor like John Ben, Hubbard also lived at Clarendon Court and proved to be JBS's closest English friend. Two years later Surefire Snow purchased a British automobile and secured a London driver's license.

A good buyer like JBS assessed the would-be consumers— their wants, needs, likes, dislikes—and overcame potential resistance. He sought new markets, especially among children and teenagers, and kept his eyes open for prospective consumers wherever he traveled. He bought as close to the market as possible and as cheaply as possible by purchasing large quantities. He also knew his product. The buyer was, in the words of master-buyer Carson Peck, "not only responsible for the purchase but for the *sale* and *profit*." Successful buyers could expect wealth, for they received large salaries plus commissions and options to buy stock from Woolworth's private reserve. As John K. Winkler pointed out in his history of the Woolworth Company, many buyers became millionaires before retirement. Such was the case of Surefire Snow.

For many years JBS bought as he traveled and traveled as he bought. His excursions through Britain took him to the large cities—Leeds, Birmingham, Liverpool, Glasgow, Edinburgh, Aberdeen, Swansea, and even to Dublin. He met with managers, especially those in new stores, and supervised openings. He dealt with salesmen and discussed new products, prices, qualities, and quantities. He bought much and he bought well.

Throughout these years JBS kept his American citizenship and retained a deep-seated loyalty to the land of his birth. Nonetheless he rarely came back to the States. During his first return in March 1913, he vacationed in New York and spent several days with his mother in Pulaski. Three years later he rushed home to attend her funeral.

On 17 September 1916 Mary Watson Snow, then in her seventy-second year, and still living in the Snow homestead in Pulaski, died suddenly. JBS received the news by cablegram the following day, secured passage on a ship that embarked from Liverpool on 20 September, and returned to Pulaski for the funeral and interment. He then remained in his hometown for several days to take care of matters pertaining to the estate and to make arrangements for his cousins to occupy the Snow homestead on Mill Street.

Shortly after his return to London, the United States joined Britain in the war against Germany and the Central Powers. Woolworth's did not suffer greatly from the war, although the naval blockade did have an adverse effect and some stores in Germany were closed. In fact, during the war years Surefire Snow and others increased sales from existing stores and continued their policy of opening new ones, so that by 1919 there were eighty-one stores in the British Isles. The war produced problems, of course, for it cut off imports from Germany and Austria and precipitated personnel difficulties because of military conscription, but these problems were alleviated by importing more items from the United States and by bringing in women and Americans as managers. None of the forty-four stores operating in England, Wales, Scotland, and Ireland on the eve of the war was forced to close. All in all, the British branch of Woolworth's weathered the war years exceptionally well.

During the immediate postwar era the British branch expanded at a faster rate than the American. Factories were converted from the production of war materiel to the manufacture of retail commodities. JBS and his fellow buyers "Bought Britain" wherever possible. But British industry could not supply all the items in demand; therefore, as they had before the war, the buyers began to import more from the Continent and from as far away as Japan.

Surefire Snow played a significant role in the expansion that characterized the postwar decade. During these affluent years the Woolworth executives occupied richly furnished offices in Victory House on Kingsway. In 1920, after Byron Miller returned to America to become vice president of Woolworth International, JBS became superintendent of buyers and reported directly to Fred Woolworth, the managing director of the British company. However, when Fred died in 1923, he was succeeded by the first British CEO, William Stephenson, rather than an American. This policy, which precluded John Ben Snow's assuming the highest post, remained in force through World War II and after.

Nonetheless, as the superintendent of buyers, JBS had broad supervisory authority over a team of buyers, mostly British, who traveled throughout the world in search of commodities and suppliers. The position entailed considerable traveling, especially in Europe and the British Isles. In the 1920s he took at least one extended buying trip each year to the Continent, normally in March, and sometimes another in later summer, generally to the Netherlands, Germany, and Czechoslovakia, all countries which had supplied Woolworth's before the war. In the 1930s Surefire's travels tapered off somewhat due to the Great Depression and the campaign to "Buy Britain," though he went to Paris several times between 1932 and 1937. Indeed, according to onetime buyer Charles McCarthy, JBS flew on the first paying passenger flight from Croydon to the Aerodrome in Paris with his friend, James Silberman, a musician and publisher.

JBS commanded great respect from his subordinates. Scotsman Kenneth Erskine, a onetime buyer, considered

Johnny Snow to be "the best American in the business." He selected good men and then gave them a free rein. He was lacking in some of the social graces deemed important in English circles, Erskine admitted, and was always "a man's man." But in his business dealings Johnny Snow was always "up and up" and "scrupulously fair." Most important, "He was a wonderful fellow."

Charles McCarthy, a Dubliner, remembered his boss as "the most tireless man I ever met." JB, as Mac called him, never stopped; he enjoyed a challenge; he thrived on adversity; he invariably took the bull by the horns. At the same time, despite this rugged individualism, JB was a team man. Mac proudly recalled how JB nearly cornered the market on popular musical scores ("sixpenny pops") during World War I, how as a complete novice he bought his first horse at an auction and then hired a groom to give him riding lessons, how he always smoked cigars, ordered large-sized clothes, had steak and sauterne at the Peahen Inn in St. Albans, and how he searched the fairs of Europe for china, dolls, and celluloid toys.

For thirty years (1909-1939) the buyer from Pulaski was, for all practical purposes, a Britisher. He worked with the English, Scottish, and Irish managers of Woolworth Ltd. He sold to British consumers. He drove a Rolls Royce. He returned to the States only once after his mother's death, in May 1933, and then only long enough to celebrate his fiftieth birthday on American soil before returning to London in late June.

During the decade following the Versailles Peace Conference, the British Woolworth Company expanded over fourfold from 81 to 343 stores. New stores opened at a rate of one every eighteen days. Sales increased proportionately. By the end of the decade the British branch was turning in better earnings and profits than the American branch. During the tenure of William Stephenson the company became more Anglicized. The directors moved the executive suite and central offices to New Bond House and changed from a private limited to a public company. In 1931 the American holdings were reduced from two-thirds to about one-half of the stock.

By the time of his retirement in the mid-1930s, Surefire Snow was a multimillionaire. He usually invested his salary, which topped $200,000 a year, in Woolworth's common and preferred stock. Upon his return to the States in 1939, he owned over 500,000 shares of common and 50,000 shares of six percent preferred in Woolworth Ltd. He had accounts in four banks, including Rothchild's in London and the Irving Trust Company in New York, and relied heavily upon bankers for financial advice.

Surefire Snow played a significant role, though often unnoticed and anonymous, in the Yankee invasion of Britain. As a pioneering multinationalist in an international corporation, long before the words were coined, he attained his goal of becoming a successful big businessman in the expanding world of commerce. He fulfilled childhood dreams and youthful ambitions in the land from which his forebears had emigrated three centuries earlier.

IV

Sir John of Highfield Farm

The life of an American businessman in Britain, especially a staid bachelor like JBS, was not always easy. It meant long hours of work in an alien environment. It also meant sacrifice, frustration, and loneliness, despite substantial financial rewards.

Surefire Snow gave up many personal contacts with family and friends when he left the States, as well as many of his favorite American avocations, and was compelled to find British substitutes. As an athlete who thrived on competition, he was forced to relinquish baseball, football, and track, all of which he had enjoyed as a participant, and to adopt some of the English sports. In time he acquired a new set of friends—many proved dearer to him than his family—and gradually assimilated many things English. He never took to the game of cricket; however, in the course of becoming Anglicized, JBS discovered what became the dominant passion of his life—horses and horsemanship.

When he took up residence in London during World War I, JBS became part of the American colony. The center of this social circle was the American ambassador to the Court of St. James and his coterie of officials and friends. From 1912 to 1918 the ambassador was Walter H. Page, who during the war backed the formation of the American Society, an association of American businessmen who met periodically in London for social purposes. These social relationships assumed permanent form with the founding of the American Club on October 12, 1918, just prior to the

Armistice, when a group of Americans including JBS met in the Savoy Hotel to establish an organization and secure a suitable building for dining, club meetings, and guest accommodations. On the following Fourth of July the American Club opened its doors at 95 Picadilly to a select number of members. Ten days later the new ambassador, John W. Davis, an honorary member of the club, hosted a formal dinner attended by JBS and his fellow founders.

JBS reaped untold benefits from his association with the American Club and took great pride in his role as a founder. It served as his home-away-from-home for twenty years. Many of the two hundred resident members—Americans residing in London—as well as some of the associate members—Britishers with American connections—became a part of his enlarging circle of friends. As one might expect, the club included many Woolworth executives, both American and English, so that the business and social circles of JBS intersected at several points. The club also gave JBS the opportunity to meet famous people from both sides of the Atlantic: the Duke of Windsor, who lunched there and was an honorary member when he ascended the throne as Edward VIII; Winston Churchill, who spoke at the club on several occasions; Prime Minister David Lloyd George; American-born Lady Astor, who in 1919 became the first woman member of the House of Commons; Will Rogers, the American actor and humorist; and countless others.

Through the American Club JBS became accustomed to the amenities of English life. He never enjoyed teas, nor did he acquire the accent of the Establishment; but he learned to enjoy haute cuisine, Cuban cigars, port wine, and French champagne. More important, through fellow members of the club he became attracted to life in the English countryside and particularly such rural sports as horseback riding, fox hunting, polo, thoroughbred breeding, and steeplechasing. He also acquired the traditional English fondness for all kinds of animals, especially horses. Thereafter the horse was JBS's first love.

JBS became so enamored of horses and of equine sports that in 1923 he acquired his own stud farm, Highfield Manor, a country estate ideally situated about thirty miles north of London near the county town of Hertford. To the west was Hatfield House, the ancestral estate of the Cecil family; to the east Hoddesdon, home of Major George Smith-Bosanquet, a well-known master of the hounds. Here Surefire Snow mastered the art of equitation, and Highfield fast became his pride, his joy, his means of relaxation, his source of inner strength.

Surefire Snow became so attached to his idyllic retreat that he featured it in his Christmas cards on several occasions. One greeting included an attractive multi-colored map depicting Highfield Farm and the roads leading to it from London.

In 1923 he sent out a calendar with a message alluding to Highfield:

> God reste ye merrie
> gentlefolke throughout
> the New Year and keep
> ye fitte and stronge to
> ryde ye Indian ponyies
> and playe ye Anciente
> Gayme of Polo atte
> Highfield Farm
> Hertford.

The stables at Highfield, large enough to board more than twenty horses, dominated the landscape. Rising above the two-story pavilion was a wooden clock tower crowned with a fox-shaped weather vane. A latticed balcony around the middle of the tower allowed onlookers a panoramic view of the grounds, fields, and wooded countryside. Nearby were the living quarters. JBS erected a comfortable Spanish-style bungalow for himself and a guest house for his friends. To the property he added a patio, shrubs and plantings, a formal garden, stone walks, and a tennis court. Scattered throughout the gardens were life-size sculptures of deer, dogs, foxes, and rabbits, all reflecting his love of animals. Surrounding the stables and grounds were several fields enclosed with white fences. To the north were fields for polo, pacing, and jumping; to the south, fields for riding and pasture. The encircling woods, though not brimming with game, served well for hunting purposes.

To Highfield came JBS's Woolworth associates, fellow members of the American Club, horse lovers from other shires, and visiting friends from the States. For the timid there were riding and jumping; for the robust there was polo; for the novice donkey polo. And for all there were drinks, food, and good company. On weekends and holidays JBS, ever generous, opened the gates of Highfield and offered hospitality in the manner of an English squire or a knight of the shire. Small wonder that he soon acquired several new appellations. He remained JB to his secretary and most Woolworth associates. But to many country folk he became John B. Snow, *Esquire*—translated "Squire Snow." To his trainer George Beeby and his groom Maurice Head, he was "the Guv'nor." One American friend, Bill Feick, affectionately dubbed him "Sir John."

When it came to horses, Sir John demanded and received the best in Britain from Waltham on the Wolds near Melton Mowbray in Leicestershire. Here in the heartland of fox hunting and thoroughbred horses, he secured from Harry Beeby, one of England's best trainers and judges of horses, a steady supply of polo ponies and horses for both hunting and racing. For many years JBS boarded his racing horses at Beeby's training stables at Waltham and kept his polo ponies at Highfield. Harry Beeby served as adviser and supplier of thoroughbreds until his death in 1935. Equally important, Sir John obtained the services of George Beeby, Harry's son, and retained him on an annual salary. George trained JBS's horses, arranged for the transportation of horses to and from Highfield, played polo on JBS's team, and rendered invaluable advice and assistance on horse breeding. He became Sir John's steward, his confidant, his lifelong friend. Even when George moved the training

*Aerial view of Highfield Stud Farm,
JBS's country home near Hertford, England*

Tennis court and polo field at Highfield Farm

Dining room at Highfield Farm

Den at Highfield Farm

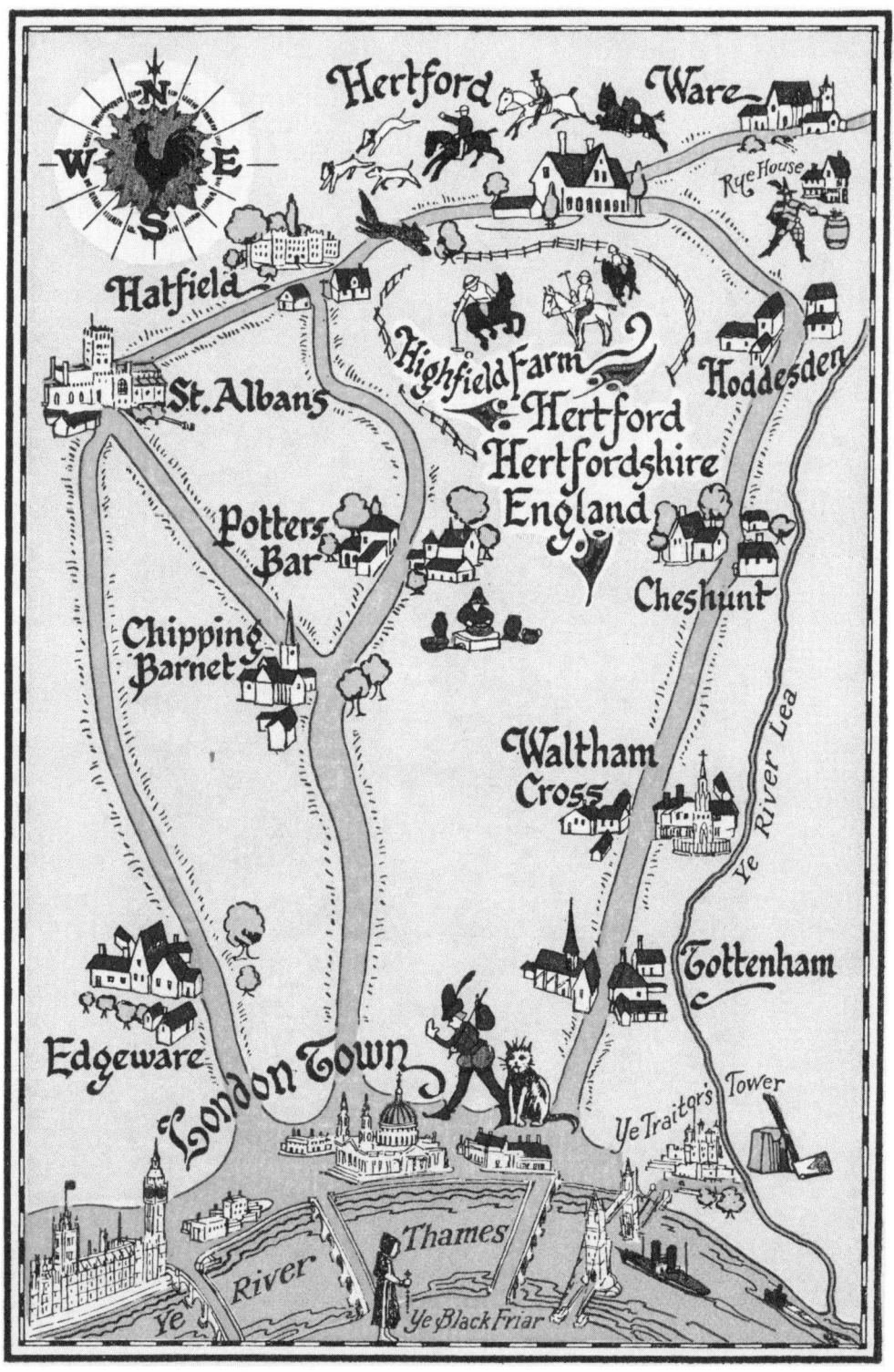

JBS Christmas card featuring Highfield Farm

JBS mounted at Highfield Farm

JBS and polo teammates at Highfield Farm

Polo match at Highfield Farm

Polo match at Highfield Farm

JBS mounted for foxhunt (1935)

JBS and lady friends at foxhunt (1936)

JBS and female friend at foxhunt (1936)

stables from Waltham to Compton in Berkshire after his father's death, he continued to serve the master of Highfield Farm.

Sir John's favorite pastime at Highfield Farm was without doubt playing polo. The layout of the grounds and the social calendar centered on this vigorous, competitive sport that had been brought to Britain from India in the previous century. JBS had a regulation-size field and the required number (sixteen) of polo ponies for a match, and the players and spectators came from his enlarging circle of English and Anglo-American friends. On special occasions such as the annual challenge match, scores of people motored to Highfield to cheer the players and enjoy Squire Snow's hospitality.

The inner circle of polo enthusiasts included George Beeby; E. C. Prescott, one of JBS's closest friends and a buyer at Woolworth's; J. M. Strausner, a fellow founder of the American Club; J. Elwell, a well-known horse trainer from Melton Mowbray; and J. Plunkett, an officer of His Majesty's Army. Harry Beeby, though aging, came from Waltham on the Wolds to referee the matches, and A. B. Carey, a close friend and officer of the American Club, sometimes served as timekeeper and scorer. Three of these horsemen—Snow, Strausner and Carey—became known as "the Three Musketeers" in Highfield Farm circles. All three were bachelor-businessmen; all lived in London where they frequented the American Club; all enjoyed horses and riding. Together they rode, feasted, attended the races, and played polo at Highfield. Occasionally they took their ponies to Melton Mowbray and played with Britain's best polo players. In 1936, as one news account described it, "A beautiful string of twelve polo ponies belonging to Mr. John Snow, one of the best-known polo enthusiasts in this country and America, arrived at Melton Mowbray on Saturday. Mr. Snow is to play on the Melton Mowbray Club's grounds at Brentingby." The twelve ponies had been brought to England from Texas ranches.

In 1929 Sir John established his annual challenge match

at Highfield. The winning team received a rotating trophy, the Highfield Challenge Cup, and each member of the team received a sterling silver cup to commemorate the victory. The match, usually held late in the summer, was followed by champagne toasts and a sumptuous repast, which invariably included oysters, steak and ice cream. On one occasion JBS imported from the States dozens of broad-brimmed sombreros and kerchiefs for the spectators, and he playfully dubbed his fellow horse lovers the Texas Rangers. On another occasion he brought down from Melton Mowbray a string of donkeys for a game of donkey polo. This humorous reversal of roles permitted the polo pros to stand and cheer while the spectators sat on their donkeys and played the game. One can almost hear JBS's boisterous shout, "Three rousing cheers!"

Always highly disciplined, Sir John developed a rigorous routine at Highfield. Each Friday afternoon he drove in his Rolls Royce from Clarendon Court to Highfield for a weekend of horseback riding. Upon arriving, he would quickly change into his riding clothes, ride for several hours, shower, and then enjoy a late dinner and champagne. According to Geoffrey Head, son of the groom, "He would dress in his cowboy outfit complete with 10 gal. Stetson and chaps, and ride around the quiet countryside around Goose Green smoking a big cigar." On Saturdays there was polo practice. Or if the weather was inclement, JBS would mount his mechanical horse located in a shed at the north end of the polo field and practice for hours with both mallet and ball. Normally his friends from Woolworth's and polo enthusiasts from other clubs would congregate in preparation for the match on the following day.

Geoffrey Head reports:

> On Sundays there would usually be a polo match with many people walking from Hoddesdon to watch. . . . My first duty was to hand out the polo sticks for most players. At the end of the chukkas I used to assist my father with JB's horses. I remember his favorite was an old horse of 13-16 years called "Crinkle," so called

because he had a bent ear. At the end of the game I used to take Crinkle and the other horses for a gentle cooling walk to Jepps farm and back. . . . During the evening a party would be held on the lawns and tennis court of the bungalow and many is the time I used to creep back and watch through the paling fence the scene of champagne corks popping and waiters dressed as cowboys serving guests.

To supervise the social activities, Sir John turned to a young Frenchwoman, Jeanne Grenier. No one knows when or how she became part of his life, but it is clear that she managed the household of Highfield. She prepared JBS's meals when he ate there and acted as hostess when he entertained. She bought the food and drink and arranged for its preparation. "The Mademoiselle" enjoyed Highfield and spent much time there according to Head "but for reasons of propriety, used to sleep in a room set aside in the farmhouse of Jepps Farm." JBS enjoyed her company, this much is certain, for photographs depict her riding and hunting at his side. He allowed her to name his race horses, hence their French names of Delaneige, Delarue, and Delapaix, and he took her to the races. He provided her with a powder blue Lincoln Continental, which she used for shopping in Hoddesdon, and prior to his departure from England JBS gave Mlle. Grenier a block of securities. One wonders whether he loved her or ever proposed marriage. She remained unmarried and died in France in December 1972 shortly before the death of JBS.

The American visitors to Highfield included Dorothy Moody, only daughter of Harry Moody, the associate of F. W. Woolworth who had advised and encouraged JBS years earlier. Moody had retired in 1918 and devoted himself to community affairs. He and his wife Anna Belle, the daughter of Isaac Douglas, lived at their charming country estate in Pulaski. On two occasions Dorothy, a horse fancier, visited Highfield Farm and long recalled riding horses from JBS's thoroughbred stables and driving in his Rolls Royce. In 1919 JBS entertained his longtime friend, Merritt Speidel, who had moved from Port Jervis to Piqua, Ohio, and then Iowa City, in each case as editor-publisher of the local newspaper. He had corresponded with JBS over the years and, more important, relied upon JBS for funds to finance his newspaper enterprises. JBS welcomed Speidel enthusiastically, taking him to Melton Mowbray and introducing him to Harry Beeby. Together they rode horseback over the fields of Highfield and traveled through the midlands in a large touring car. It was a memorable reunion for both and cemented the bond of friendship between them.

For a bachelor business executive, these athletic activities and the social life at Highfield meant people, conviviality, friendships—welcome alternatives to the monotony and loneliness of a familyless existence. Hitherto JBS had paid little attention to women and less to the thought of marriage. He never overcame a deep-seated distrust of the domineering woman. But at Highfield he hosted horse lovers of both sexes. He befriended and rode with the wives and women friends of his riding companions. According to Mrs. Laura Hayward, he dated actresses, generally after his Thursday evening at the theater, and loved musicals and dances; in fact, Mrs. Hayward had been one of his close friends during and after World War I. In England Sir John enjoyed the cheers and company of women but continued to avoid matrimony.

The stag hunts that had brought Queen Elizabeth and King James I to the vicinity of Highfield in the sixteenth and seventeenth centuries had long since been replaced by the highly stylized fox hunt. By 1920 England was divided into hunting territories and each area had its own customs and its leader, the master of the hounds. Sir John's neighbor, Major George Smith-Bosanquet of Broxbronebury Park near Hoddesdon, presided over the hunts in the Hertford area. A retired army officer who had served in the Boer War and an experienced master of the hounds, Smith-Bosanquet had won national reputation for using a pack of bitches instead of hounds. Evidently he held JBS in high esteem, for in 1937 he extended to his neighbor special hunting privileges on his estate. Among the ninety-odd members of the major's hunt were Viscount Cranborne (heir to the Marquess of Salisbury), the archdeacon of St. Albans, Sir Hugh Trenchard, Sir Brodie Henderson, a few army officers and several unmarried women. All the participants wore the appropriate garb: black top hats, white shirts or blouses, black riding coats, white breeches, and high black boots.

In 1925 Sir John became a member of Smith-Bosanquet's hunt; thereafter he paid his annual dues of £50 and hunted in the same forests that England's ruling elite had hunted in for centuries. On one occasion he hunted in the Quorm Hunt, the best known in the midlands; similarly he participated in the exclusive Enfield Chace Foxhound Hunt, patronized by many lords and ladies, and attended the Enfield Chace Ball held at Bedwell Park. On several of these fox hunts he escorted Mlle. Grenier. His favorite riding horse bore the name of George Washington.

The horses of Highfield and the social life they generated transformed JBS from a staid and slow-speaking merchandiser to a sparkling and sportive gentleman. Polo and hunting demanded physical prowess, courage, a competitive spirit, and an understanding of horses, plus skill and experience in riding, all of which he possessed. In particular, polo was good for JBS, for it brought out the virility of the player. It made a man of small stature larger than both man and horse and bolstered his ego. It thus enabled the inner man to conquer the outer man, like the legend of Pegasus encouraging the horseman to fly onward and upward to new and different worlds beyond the reach of earthbound man. Fittingly JBS had inscribed in stone above the fireplace in the lounge at Highfield Farm his motto: KEEP ON SOARING.

It was a short jump from fox hunting to horse racing in the England of George V. Sir John made that jump several years after acquiring Highfield Farm and became an avid patron of the turf, focusing his interest not in flat racing or trotting but in steeplechasing. This interest stemmed from his fox hunting, just as the sport itself evolved, for the steeplechase was a simulated and glorified fox hunt with the inclusion of man-made hazards and spectators. The steeplechase relied upon the same type of horse, a thoroughbred jumper, and required similar training plus stamina. Just as the hunting horse raced through open fields and jumped over streams, fallen trees, fences, and hedgerows in pursuit of the fox, so the steeplechaser galloped several miles and jumped over ditches, canals, and artificial gorse fences. There was no track but instead a thick green turf, frequently wet and slippery, with hazards at every turn.

Nevertheless, steeplechasing differed from fox hunting in two respects: it was much more dangerous for the rider and much more demanding of the horse. Most patrons of the turf did not ride their own steeds; rather they relied upon slight featherweight jockeys to race their thoroughbreds. The jockeys were professionals—experienced, skilled, and organized. The sport of steeplechasing was in fact highly organized and centralized. For the riders there was a Jockey Club; for the steeplechase course owners, the Turf Authority; for the breeders, a national registry; for the patrons (owners), the National Hunt Club, with many customs and a growing body of regulations.

Sir John of Highfield became a member of the National Hunt Club and from 1928 to 1938 raced in hundreds of steeplechase meetings, his orange and blue colors contrasting sharply with the verdant turf. He did not attend his first horse race until December 1928, when Delarue was running at Sandown, and then had the pleasure of witnessing his first victory. JBS differed from most patrons in that he worked day in and day out while his rivals lived lives of leisure. As one sports commentator noted: "He is a very hard worker and can never go to a meeting except on Saturdays. He is an ideal type of owner, though, as he has only one ambition, which is to win." Win or not, JBS acquired a national reputation. "Mr. Snow is a great sportsman," wrote one English columnist. "It must be a delight to train for a man of this type. Beeby is most fortunate in his patrons."

Even though Sir John began buying and breeding jumpers before 1928, he did not become a real challenger and threat until several years later. To participate in the races sponsored by the National Hunt, he needed thoroughbreds, that is, horses registered in the British Stud Book, the official record kept by Weatherby and Sons. JBS acquired his thoroughbreds from the stables of Harry and George Beeby. He obtained the services of Weatherby and Sons to keep his books, pay his entrance fees, receive his winnings, and disburse expenses. He employed George Beeby as his trainer and Jack Moloney as his regular jockey.

Sir John renamed all his thoroughbred racing horses by giving them the French prefix *de la*. His early victories came with Delarue, which won the Sandown Handicap in 1928 and the Strayer's Handicap at Cheltenham one year later. He named his favorite horse, a brown gelding by Santair, Delaneige, meaning "belonging to Snow." Delaneige ran in two Grand Nationals, finishing second to Miss Paget's Golden Miller in one and fourth to Kellsboro' Jack in the other. He ran in three Sefton races, winning one, finishing second in the other two. He steeplechased those nineteen miles with Moloney as his jockey and without a fall. In the words of *The Field*, "He may be considered one of the best horses which have gone to post." In 1933 Delaneige won the Nottingham Handicap, the Ewell Handicap at Sandown Park, and the Penkridge Chase at Wolverhampton. The following year he took first in the Prince of Wales Handicap at Sandown and placed second in four other races including the Grand National. He ran the last in record time (9.23) but still came in second to Golden Miller. In 1935 he won the Little Go Chase at Manchester and the Sefton Chase at Liverpool. JBS also owned and raced Delachance, Delagrande, Delapaix, Delavilla, Delagrace, Delaglance, and Delaferme. For over a decade these horses crisscrossed Britain with their trainer in quest of wins in England's leading steeplechases.

The premier race, the Grand National, generally met toward the end of the steeplechasing season at Aintree Club, five miles north of Liverpool. Sir John's steeplechasers ran in many Grand Nationals. They came close to winning, placing second, fourth and fifth, and won their owner much attention and acclaim, but none of his Delas ever took first place. They won him first and prize money at Sandown, Cheltenham, Lingfield, Sefton, and several other well-known races, but they denied him a decade-long ambition of winning the world's longest and most hazardous steeplechase. This is not to fault Sir John's steeds, for they confronted some of the keenest competition in the century-old history of steeplechasing.

Though falling short of his grand ambition, Sir John kept his racing ledger in the black. Omitting the original cost of the thoroughbred horses and treating them as a capital investment, the receipts from his winning purses exceeded the disbursements each year. When he returned to the States in 1939 after a decade of competition, JBS showed a surplus of slightly over $1,000. Out of his winnings he had paid annual retainers to Beeby, a salary plus 10 percent of each purse to Moloney, entrance fees, veterinarian bills, and bookkeeping expenses.

JBS preferred active participation to spectator sports; yet he thoroughly enjoyed steeplechasing. There were vicarious thrills in watching the galloping horses thunder by the grandstands. For the patron there was the pleasure of cheering *his* horse and *his* jockey on to victory. Both before and after the race, especially at the Grand National, the patron-owner attracted much publicity and the attention of newspaper columnists and sportscasters. For five years, from 1933 through 1938, JBS and his Delas proved very newsworthy. *The London Illustrated News* depicted Delaneige and Jack Moloney in the final stretch of the record-breaking Grand National of 1933. Even though Delaneige finished fourth out of thirty-four starters, the first four contestants to pass the finish line beat the previous best time set by Cloister in 1893. The next year JBS was featured in an article as the owner of two entries in the Grand National (Delaneige and Delachance, neither of which placed) and found himself

JBS with trainer Beeby (far right) and friends at Highfield Stud Farm (1931)

JBS at Grand National Steeplechase (1935)

JBS's favorite "Delaneige" (1933)

*Trainer Beeby, JBS and J. Moloney mounted on
"Delaneige" (1934)*

JBS's "Delaneige" and J. Moloney (1933)

Moloney on "Delaneige" taking the first fence at the Grand National (1934)

*Moloney on "Delaglace" taking the last fence
at the Sefton Steeplechase (1935)*

JBS's "Delachance" (1938)

JBS featured in cartoon (1933)

JBS as subject of racing cartoon (1936)

appearing in a humorous cartoon published in *The Tour*.

>AS FOR MR. J. B. SNOW—
>HE ASPIRES TO SUCH HEIGHTS
>THAT SOME DAY—DELANEIGE
>MAY JUMP THE MOON.

For the centenary commemoration of the Grand National in 1937, JBS also attracted the attention of the cartoonists and photographers as a possible winner. Delaneige lost his rider early in the race, and Delachance lost hers after the twenty-second fence. Only the presence of King George VI and Queen Elizabeth made the hundredth anniversary of steeplechasing a memorable event for the patron from Highfield.

News of JBS's participation in steeplechasing, particularly in the Grand Nationals, reached the States through the wire services and radio, and American horse racing fans followed his activities through newspaper accounts. In the July 1937 issue of *The Winged Foot*, the monthly periodical published by the New York Athletic Club, there appeared a short piece entitled "Snow's Horses" which highlighted the Grand National and Delaneige. In 1938 the official magazine of his fraternity, Phi Gamma Delta (shortened to Figi), featured JBS and Delachance in an article entitled "Figi Horse in the Grand National." JBS's most avid booster in America was Merritt Speidel who, as editor of the *Iowa City Press-Citizen*, made much of Surefire's steeplechasing activities. He followed them via the wire services and frequently reported them in his newspaper. In 1937 he gave a large party to celebrate JBS's anticipated victory in the Grand National, and scores of Iowans drank toasts to the horse racing fortunes of Speidel's crony. Thus the fame of Sir John spread to the plains of mid-America.

JBS's interest in steeplechasing continued long after he returned to the States. He followed the Grand National each year through *The London Illustrated News*, to which he subscribed until his death, and other magazines devoted to horsemanship and racing. From his hunting and racing companions in England he received articles and clippings. His memorabilia included photographs, trophies, letters, ledgers, and a large scrapbook featuring his steeplechasing accomplishments. He never forgot his horses, especially his beloved Delas, or the exciting days when he was a patron of the turf. Instead of answering his phone with the traditional English greeting, "Snow here," he frequently greeted the caller with a thunderous "Galloping horses."

In the world of horses, as in the world of mass merchandising, John Ben Snow aimed high and thought big. He relished contests of wit and skill even as a spectator and thrived on competition. He aimed to win, and having won some races, he aspired to win the world's greatest horse race. He trained a winner in Delaneige and then produced a string of winners. However, like Bellerophon, the mythical horseman who flew heavenward on the winged horse Pegasus, he did not succeed in attaining his highest goal. Nonetheless JBS never failed to give the British people a good race for their money.

V

The Silent Partner

On 16 June 1936, after thirty years of faithful service, JBS retired from his buyer's position with Woolworth's. He was honored with a retirement dinner, toasts, and laudatory speeches and received from his associates a handsome silver serving tray inscribed with their signatures. Later in the summer he reciprocated with a fete at Highfield Farm that included horseback riding, donkey polo, an outdoor buffet, and champagne. JBS did not, however, immediately return to America. Instead he retained his position as a director of Woolworth's and lived in England for three more years, spending fewer hours in his New Bond Street office and Clarendon Court and devoting more time to his thoroughbred horses at Highfield Farm. He also began to summer in the States and gradually to reorient his life toward a second career there.

Despite prolonged absences he had maintained contacts with several American friends and relatives. Through a subscription to the *Pulaski Democrat*, he followed local developments. Through intermittent letters, wires, and phone calls, he kept in touch with classmate Orimell Olmstead. Through his cousin Anna Caldwell, who usually spent her summers in the Snow homestead, he kept up connections with his few living relatives. He also maintained ties with several Woolworth associates, with banker friends at the Irving Trust Company, and with Merritt Speidel.

Through the years JBS gave several indications that he, like Harry Moody, would eventually retire in Pulaski. When he returned to the States in 1923, he revealed this intention to a reporter, who incorporated it in a news item. He demonstrated this intention more concretely in 1933 when he decided to rebuild the family homestead and employed Orimell Olmstead, then proprietor of the Ontario Iron Works, to supervise the project. Thus the sturdy frame house built by his grandfather in 1825 gave way to the New England colonial house that is still standing. JBS, however, never lived in it but instead allowed his cousins to reside there, for in the end he did not retire in Pulaski.

Initially JBS reestablished himself in New York City, where he had lived for several years during the first decade of the century; while in Britain he had used the Woolworth Building as his U.S. address. Consequently, in 1937 he leased a comfortable corner suite on the fifteenth floor of the Waldorf-Astoria which served as his legal residence in America for thirty years thereafter. He also became a member of the New York Athletic Club, which he used for entertainment and relaxation. *The Winged Foot* reported:

> Upon his recent return to New York, Mr. Snow came to visit his friends in the N.Y.A.C., and he found time to enjoy a work-out in the saddle of the electric horse which he donated to our gymnasium several months ago. He says that the mechanical steed provides nearly as much enjoyment and thrills as a real horse both for riding and polo playing. Mr. Snow went through the motions of swinging the mallet, with the machine geared to its highest speed—and liked it.

At about this time JBS also took up ranching in the American West, where he had heretofore never spent much time, although his brother Norman had lived in Colorado and Merritt Speidel had written about the glories of the Rocky Mountains and the Sierra Nevadas. In the West he could continue his riding and breeding of thoroughbreds and enjoy the freedom of wide open spaces. He therefore made arrangements to use the Diamond S Ranch near Cheyenne, Wyoming, and the Rancho de las Fuentes near Palo Alto, California.

The lure of the West and his ambition to launch a second career brought JBS into a closer business arrangement with Merritt Speidel—editor, publisher, civic leader. Decades before in Port Jervis the two men had talked about building a large chain of newspapers. Speidel's grandiose plan had called for a total of forty-eight newspapers, one in each state.

JBS had always demonstrated an interest in the printed word. At the Pulaski Academy he had worked on the student newspaper and annual. At NYU he had served as editor of the campus paper. He was an avid reader of newspapers and magazines, both in England and America, subscribing to several dailies and many weeklies. Nonetheless he had no formal training in journalism and, except for his student endeavors, could claim no experience as a reporter, correspondent, editor, or publisher. Moreover, he knew little or nothing about the technical aspects of printing. On the other hand, he always read the printed word carefully; he possessed a critical eye for news reporting and editing; and he had a practical knowledge of accounting, finance, and corporate organization. Most important JBS knew what he did not know.

In contrast, Speidel was a lifelong newspaperman. He knew the business from the inside. He had demonstrated a remarkable aptitude for journalism while a teenager in Port Jervis, and he could claim wide experience as a reporter, city editor, national correspondent, business manager, and publisher. He had written articles for the Associated Press, the *New York Times*, and the *New York Herald Tribune*. He had valuable connections with civic organizations, editors and publishers, the Republican Party, and with several Presidents and their campaign managers. Furthermore, Speidel possessed great ambitions and endless drive.

* * *

The Snow-Speidel partnership began in 1909 with the purchase of a relatively small newspaper in northern Ohio.

JBS, already a successful merchandiser with Woolworth's, supplied the capital to finance the purchase of the *Piqua Daily Call*. Speidel, then manager of the *Port Jervis Daily Union*, provided the know-how, the connections, the day-by-day leadership. About the time that Snow departed for Britain, Speidel moved to Ohio and, as the ebullient editor-publisher, transformed the *Piqua Daily Call* into one of the state's most influential newspapers. Snow assumed the inconspicuous role, which he apparently relished, of a silent partner and played the part so well that no one, not even Speidel's family, learned the details of the partnership until three decades later.

In 1921 Speidel sold the Piqua newspaper and, again with the backing of his silent partner in London, purchased the *Iowa City Press-Citizen*. He expanded circulation, increased the advertising, and built up an organization of competent and ambitious newspapermen, many of whom had ties with the University of Iowa's School of Journalism. He became deeply involved in civic affairs and established himself as a public-spirited leader of the community. During the economic crises of 1932, when several Iowa City banks closed, Speidel secured financial assistance from his silent partner, organized a new bank (the First Capital National Bank), and served as a director. Speidel took credit for the restoration of banking in Iowa City, but Snow had provided the emergency capital of several hundred thousand dollars in cash.

Though separated by thousands of miles, the Snow-Speidel partnership matured and flourished. The two men kept in touch periodically. Speidel wrote long florid letters, actually informal reports, packed with details about himself, his growing family, and the status of their secret venture. JBS responded with crisp cablegrams, an occasional snapshot or newspaper clipping, and an annual Christmas greeting. If not completely silent, partner Snow was a man of few written words. The meetings between the two were infrequent and brief. The first occurred in 1923 when, after visiting Pulaski, JBS traveled to Iowa City and spent a few days with the Speidel family. Ten years later he celebrated his fiftieth birthday in Iowa with Speidel. During that visit JBS was honored by the Iowa City Council of Boy Scouts and thanked for his generous gifts to the organization. Meanwhile in 1929 Speidel visited Highfield and toured England with Snow. Gradually Speidel's youthful dream of a large chain of newpapers became a reality.

The financial mechanics of the Snow-Speidel partnership defy easy explanation. Drawing from his lucrative salary, dividend income, and credit, JBS transferred large amounts of cash to Speidel, who in turn used the money to buy a newspaper, improve a plant, or invest until the opportune moment. JBS treated the transaction as a loan and charged Speidel one percent interest per annum. Speidel paid the interest annually, depositing the sums in an Iowa City bank account which he opened for his silent partner. In brief, Speidel became Snow's steward. He received and invested the funds, deposited the dividends from JBS's share of stock in a joint account, made philanthropic contributions in JBS's name, exercised his proxy in business meetings, and forwarded data to JBS's tax experts in New York. And each year he submitted an accounting of his stewardship to his silent partner.

Thus Snow made possible the realization of Speidel's dream, for in addition to the *Piqua Daily Call* (1909) and the *Iowa City Press-Citizen* (1921), his funds were used to purchase the *Chillicothe Scioto Gazette* (1935), the *Salinas Index-Journal* (1936), and the *Salinas Post* (1936). By this time Speidel more realistically envisioned a transcontinental chain of twelve newspapers, each in a different state, reaching across mid-America. The acquisition rate accelerated in the years following JBS's retirement. In quick succession he supplied funds to purchase the *Fort Collins Express-Courier* (1936), the *Chillicothe News Advertiser* (1938), the Cheyenne Newspapers, Incorporated (1939), the *Poughkeepsie Sunday Courier* (1939), and two Reno newspapers the same year.

JBS emerged from his role as silent partner slowly and

inconspicuously. At the annual meeting of shareholders of the *Iowa City Press-Citizen*, usually involving only five people, his name appeared on the books as a major shareholder, and he was elected chairman of the board. His proxy was exercised by Speidel, who served as vice chairman, president, and executive officer. The same pattern of organization prevailed in Chillicothe, Salinas, and Fort Collins, so that by 1937 JBS headed, in absentia, four newspapers. In August of that year the Snow-Speidel team formed a holding company, a super-management organization, to purchase additional newspapers and to centralize the business operations of existing enterprises. JBS became chairman of the board and supplied the necessary funds. Shortly thereafter Speidel moved from Iowa City to Palo Alto, where he established the central offices of the newly formed organization.

Though JBS continued to shun publicity, he allowed his name to be associated with such civic organizations as the Rotary Club of Iowa City, and he permitted the Boy Scouts to name a cabin after him in their camp near Iowa City. He did not, however, want his name attached to the newly formed holding company; instead it became Speidel Newspapers, Incorporated (SNI). And he would not allow his name to appear on the masthead or stationery of any of the newspapers. When Speidel attempted to bring him from backstage into the limelight, as he did several times, silent Snow remained adamant and declined all recognition.

The disagreement between Snow and Speidel over publicity did not disrupt the close relationship between them. On the contrary, their friendship ripened with the passing years. Each summer after 1936 JBS returned to the States and spent time with the Speidels. The two men enjoyed recalling their youth and looking forward to the completion of their transcontinental chain of newspapers. Thus in 1938 Speidel induced his silent partner to spend Christmas with him and his family in Palo Alto. This was JBS's first Christmas in the States since 1909 and his first with the Speidel family. It proved to be a warm and memorable occasion with much conversation, eating, singing, and exchanging of gifts. By New Year's Day JBS was part of the family.

Shortly after the first of the year, JBS responded with an unprecedented act of generosity: he gave his longtime friend and partner fifty thousand shares of Woolworth common stock worth roughly $1,000,000. For once in his life, after receiving what he called "The Magnificent Million," Merritt Speidel was at a loss for words to express his appreciation. As events would prove, Speidel was merely the first of many men who owed their first million to the liberality of John Ben Snow.

* * *

Meanwhile, on 3 September 1939, the British government declared war on Nazi Germany as a consequence of the aggressive actions of Adolf Hitler. When war broke out, JBS had been in the States for several months making plans with Merritt Speidel for his second career. He had intended to return to Britain in the autumn, resign his directorship at Woolworth's, liquidate his businesses, sell his property, and then transfer his holdings to New York—all in preparation for resettlement in the States. In fact, he already had his reservation to sail.

The outbreak of hostilities, especially on the Atlantic Ocean, disrupted his plans. His initial reaction was to sail according to schedule, but upon learning that the British ship *Athenia* had been sunk by a German submarine, he wired his secretary Mabel Jenkins, "What shall I do?" After discussing the matter with others at Woolworth House, she wired back, "Stay where you are; it is not safe crossing." JBS then abandoned his travel plans, stayed in the States, and submitted his letter of resignation. The board of directors thereupon passed the following resolution:

> THAT Mr. J. B. Snow's resignation as Director of the Company, dated 30th October, 1939, be accepted with regret, and the Secretary is instructed to convey to Mr. J. B. Snow the Board's regret and their appreciation of

his past services to the Company over a period of 30 years.

The next month JBS received a handwritten letter from his old associate, W. L. Stephenson:

> I know how you must feel severing your connection with the old Firm which has meant so much to you in every way. Yet I can understand the position you find yourself in. We old timers (not so many now) feel the wrench as you do. Thirty years together is no mean part of one's span—and we certainly went through many struggles shoulder to shoulder. I shall always remember you as a most buoyant and devoted comrade —a pillar of strength in times of need.
>
> I'm glad to learn that you are really getting your teeth into the Newspaper game. You are very wise to build up something of this nature as an outlet for the energies you still possess in so large a measure.

JBS had hoped to say good-bye to his English business associates and friends in person. He had also hoped to see his horses for the last time, personally dispose of them, and arrange of the sale of Highfield. But with the outbreak of war he was forced to rely upon friends and agents; consequently, several years passed before his personal affairs in England were settled. Miss Jenkins took care of countless details, forwarding his mail, paying unsettled accounts, closing his office at Woolworth House, and shipping his papers. She also arranged for the packing and shipping of his personal possessions from Clarendon Court to New York. "J. B. wanted me to keep things running smoothly," she noted, "and I did my best but things were difficult." JBS's close friends, the Prescotts, assumed the unpleasant task of disposing of his horses and stud farm. Actually, before the transfer of Highfield was completed, the British government preempted the property to use as a training facility for the British army. The polo and riding fields became pastures; the grounds soon fell into a state of disrepair. Worse yet, most of JBS's horses, including his favorite Delaneige, were "put to sleep." Total war demanded extreme measures and sacrifice.

To manage his personal finances, JBS retained Baker and Sutton, a prestigious accounting firm that had handled his taxes for several years. This London firm, with offices also in New York, arranged for the liquidation of his three investment companies and the conversion of his holdings into American dollars and U.S. securities. They continued to take care of his complicated tax returns and arranged for the payment of some accounts and the shipment of his Rolls Royce. The taxes and transfers proved to be so complex and time-consuming that Baker and Sutton did not complete their assignment until 1942. They worked closely with the Irving Trust Company in America, the London branch of Chase National Bank, and F. W. Woolworth in the transfer of JBS's funds from England to the States. They also worked with the well-known New York law firm of Tolbert, Ewen and Patterson, particularly with the senior partner, Ward Tolbert, who had handled JBS's tax returns and given legal advice for many years. Soon Tolbert was succeeded by a younger member of the firm, Talbot Malcolm, who eventually became JBS's personal attorney, confidant, and friend.

While the labors of these people freed JBS from the irksome details involved in a transoceanic move, they did not lessen the psychological impact. It was no simple matter for him to sever his ties with England, his adopted homeland, and reestablish himself in the States. He had lived there the middle third of his long life; many of his closest friends and business associates were English; he owned property and had roots in the countryside; many of his mannerisms, habits, and tastes were English. It was not easy for a bachelor in his mid-fifties with no close relatives to change his way of life. Consequently, there were several years of trial and error before he finally settled in Colorado Springs.

Similarly it was difficult for JBS to leave Woolworth's, his surrogate family ever since the death of his mother. For nearly forty years the company had been the object of his loyalty and affection, the source of many enduring friendships, and the genesis of his fortune. While he remained a large shareholder and followed the activities of his successors through the company's publications, he had now become an outsider, a retired member of his Woolworth family. Nonetheless his loyalty to Woolworth's never faltered. He corresponded with his business associates and their widows for decades. He kept in touch with Miss Jenkins and her family until his death. He followed Woolworth's in *The New Bond*, *The Woolworth News*, and the *Wall Street Journal*. He retained and treasured many Woolworth mementos. Until his death, long after Speidel Newspapers, Inc. became his family, he cherished his connections with F. W. Woolworth and Company.

It was also difficult for JBS to sever his connections with Highfield Farm and those associated with his favorite avocation. After the war the land and stables were purchased by Merck Pharmaceutical and converted to a laboratory, while the house and gardens became the residence of Philip Nicholas, a retired real estate broker to whom JBS bore a striking resemblance. Though he never returned to Highfield, he loved to reminisce about his favorite horses, the polo matches, the foxhunts, and the parties. His memories were kept alive by the scores of mounted photographs lining the walls of his office and hotel suite and by huge scrapbooks filled with newspaper clippings. Moreover, during and after the war he kept in touch with his fellow horse fanciers by cables, letters, and greeting cards.

Shortly after Britain's declaration of war, JBS bestowed upon his English friends blocks of Woolworth securities amounting to tens of thousands of dollars. In addition to Mlle. Grenier, who had received twelve thousand shares, trainer George Beeby and polo partners Strausner and Carey each received one thousand, while L. S. Elwell, H. S. Tiel, and R. R. Chamberlain received lesser amounts. During the war JBS sent his English friends food packages and in the 1950s helped underwrite the university education of Beeby's son. Distance and time did not obliterate bonds of friendship.

JBS never returned to Britain; yet he retained many

things English for the rest of his life. He subscribed to several English magazines, including *The London Illustrated News* and *Punch*, and kept abreast of events with keen interest. Through newspaper clippings and letters from horse-loving friends, he followed the English polo matches, horse sales, steeplechases, and fox hunts. He always bought and drove the best English-made car—a Rolls Royce, of course—and invariably used his English driving gloves. His continued use of such English words as *boot* for *trunk* and *lift* for *elevator*, not to mention his pronunciation of *schedule*, reflected the influence of his thirty years in Britain.

VI

A Western Horseman

Upon returning to the States, JBS could have gone into retirement and lived on the income from his multimillion-dollar investments; but such a thought probably never occurred to him, for he thrived on an active life. He was determined to ride, breed horses, and round out his life with a second career as a newspaper executive.

He apparently considered living in Pulaski, for in addition to rebuilding the family homestead, he retained the heirlooms and closely followed village affairs. In April 1940 he revisited Pulaski, spending several days with Orimell Olmstead. However, despite a continuing interest in the village, he decided that as a place in which to resettle, Pulaski did not fit into the Snow-Speidel plan for a transcontinental chain of newspapers. Moreover, upstate New York with its long snowy winters would have afforded him insufficient opportunity to ride on a daily basis.

JBS rejected New York City for similar reasons. Though he appreciated the advantages of living near the theater and Wall Street, New York was three thousand miles from Palo Alto, the new home of the Speidels and headquarters of Speidel Newspapers, Inc. Moreover, living in a big city would have forced him to sacrifice his desire to raise cattle, breed quarter horses, and ride. He decided, nevertheless, to retain his permanent address and legal residence in New York, for he realized that he would need to return there periodically to consult with his legal and financial advisers and to vote in general elections. Thus several times each year for over twenty years he went to New York, sometimes lunching with Norman Woolworth during these visits.

Meanwhile, responding to the urging of Merritt Speidel, JBS went to the West Coast to try living in California. After staying briefly with the Speidel family, he moved to the President, a small residential hotel in Palo Alto near the offices of Speidel Newspapers. He instituted a work and exercise routine somewhat different from his routine in England, which he continued until his final illness. He rose early, rode in the morning for several hours, lunched with his associates, worked afternoons at his office in the Frazer Building, then dined at either the hotel or the Los Altos Country Club.

To best realize his ambition to breed horses and to ride regularly, JBS relied on Don and Florence Flint, a ranching couple whom he had met in Wyoming several years before. He induced the Flints to come to California, assisted them in buying a ranch north of Palo Alto on Canada Road, then worked out an arrangement that enabled him to ride whenever he wished—with the Flints, Harry Bunker, Doc Eaton, and new friends and business associates. Foremost among these new friends was avid horseman and rancher, Bob Holliday, a San Francisco advertising executive. He and JBS rode together, especially at Holliday's ranch near Hollister, talked horses hours upon end, and cooperated in the training and breeding of saddle horses.

Through Holliday's connections, JBS became a member of Rancheros Visitadores, an exclusive horse-lovers club with headquarters in Santa Barbara. Each member was expected to be an expert rider and horse fancier. Each year the members gathered for their annual trek, an organized trail ride, in the Sierra Nevada Mountains. All riders were expected to wear their Stetsons, ties, belts, buckles, and pins —all decorated with the symbol R_V, official insignia of the Rancheros Visitadores. JBS benefited immensely from these new associations. His circle of horse fanciers expanded, and the Rancheros served as a substitute for his fox hunts in England. He took great pride in his membership in the club, treasured his R_V garb, and cherished his friendships with Holliday and fellow Visitadores long after he left California.

JBS gave up polo when he returned to America but never lost his interest in the game. He followed the activities of the English matches through magazines; he subscribed to and read the official newssheet of the U.S. Polo Association. He filled his office walls with photographs of the Highfield matches and his furniture with silver cup trophies. The clinching evidence of his prowess, however, remained his viselike handshake—a handshake that never ceased to amaze the unwary greeter. He loved to demonstrate that he hadn't lost his "grasp" of the game.

JBS found a suitable substitute for polo and racing in the rodeo and horse shows. Just as he had once attended the Cheyenne Rodeo as a spectator when in Wyoming, so he frequented the California Rodeo held annually in Salinas. To Salinas came the West's best broncs, ropers, and wranglers, as well as aficionados like Will Rogers, one of JBS's heroes. One year he sat with Governor Frank Merriam in the VIP box, an honor arranged by Merritt Speidel. In 1940 he was named honorary director of the California Rodeo. After settling in Colorado Springs, he never missed the Pikes' Peak or Bust Rodeo, often leading the parade as grand marshal.

His interest in ranching was a means to an end, for his first love remained horses and horseback riding. He dressed the role of the rancher-cowboy, to be sure, with his Stetson, tapered shirt, bolo tie, and high-heeled boots. He won election to the Cowboy Hall of Fame. He showed some interest in breeding and in cattle raising, but he never owned a ranch or paid taxes on a piece of land. "I'm not a rancher," he freely confessed; "I simply love horses." JBS did not ride for a living; rather he lived for riding.

* * *

In December 1941, in response to the attack upon Pearl Harbor, the United States declared war on Japan and joined Britain in the struggle against Nazi Germany. JBS remained pro-British and sympathetic with the war aims. Except for inconveniences, the war had little direct impact on his life. Nonetheless he became involved in an embarrassing situation resulting from a wartime political controversy.

In New York there was a rabid anti-Roosevelt and pro-German organization known as the League for Constitutional Government, founded in the early 1930s and headed by one John B. Snow, a controversial speaker and writer. During the early years of World War II, the pro-Fascist connections of this John B. Snow were investigated and exposed in the press, particularly the New York tabloids, which portrayed him as a traitor. Though residing in a Park Avenue apartment, he ran the League from an office directly across the street from the Waldorf-Astoria and occasionally cashed checks in that hotel. In addition, his signature bore a striking resemblance to that of JBS.

So great was JBS's irritation that he instructed his attorney, Ward Tolbert, to recommend some course of action. He had always been proud of his name, especially his surname, and hypersensitive about derogatory publicity. The possibility of being mistakenly identified as a pro-Fascist whose activities bordered on treason evoked an anguished plea from JBS. During his investigation Tolbert discovered to his dismay that there were three midtown New Yorkers with the name John B. Snow. The third, John *Bernard* Snow, likewise embarrassed by the adverse publicity, had already moved away. "We have taken up residence in South Carolina which may lessen the confusion for all concerned," he wrote Tolbert. "For any further communication our address is Orange Grove Plantation, Frogmore, South Carolina."

Upon receiving this communication from John Bernard Snow, Tolbert wrote JBS a letter dated 17 April 1943:

> Dear John:
>
> In answer to our recent letter written to John B. Snow at 45 Park Avenue, I received a letter which I am herewith enclosing. The matter is still a mystery

because there is apparently a third John B. Snow. I never heard of so many John B. Snows. Are they all named after you, or is it a name a lot of people like? In any event, what will we do now? I might advise you to change your name to John Pelham Snow; besides being distinctive that would have a meaning, because of the horse named Pelham. Although our letter was addressed to John B. Snow at 45 Park Avenue, we get a reply on a letterhead bearing the address 277 Park Avenue. When you come east the next time we [had] better get a detective and find out who John B. Snow is — or better said, who they are.

Yours sincerely,
Ward B. Tolbert

JBS did not regard it as a laughing matter and in fact could not talk about it decades later without extreme agitation. Nevertheless, he did follow Tolbert's advice and changed his middle name, thereby eradicating all confusion. Though the name Benjamin had been his father's, henceforth JBS's middle name would be Ben, and he would be known as, not John Snow, not John B. Snow, not John Benjamin Snow, but John *Ben* Snow.

* * *

In mid-March 1942, after nearly two years in California, JBS moved to Colorado Springs. Because the war adversely affected both transcontinental mail and train service, the Speidel executives decided to relocate their offices in a more central place. JBS had visited Colorado Springs years before and liked it; moreover, his friends Don and Florence Flint, who had lived there, convinced him of its superiority over Palo Alto as a place to live, ride, and work, especially in wartime. Thus the entire Speidel organization moved there, and though Merritt Speidel and his family returned to Palo Alto toward the end of the war, JBS stayed in Colorado Springs for the rest of his life. He initially leased a suite in the Antlers Hotel, conveniently located in the central city, remaining as a permanent guest until it was razed to make way for the present Antlers, then moved to the Mayfair Motel. He also joined the El Paso Club, an exclusive dining and social club, and remained a dedicated member until his death. In the absence of a home, these institutions provided him with the day-by-day amenities and personal services to which he had become accustomed in England.

Meanwhile Speidel Newspapers secured offices on the top floor of the Mining Exchange Building. Here, in the corner room overlooking Pike's Peak Avenue and Nevada Streets, JBS presided over his "family," with Harry Bunker, his loyal financial expert, in an office to his left and Beryl Eaton, his private secretary, in an office to his right adjacent to the reception room. For over thirty years JBS spent many hours each day, seven days each week, in the Mining Exchange Building. His coming and going proved so predictable that legendary stories circulated among local merchants and townspeople regarding his routine.

To assure himself a place for riding and breeding horses, JBS again assisted the Flints in the purchase of a ranch about fifteen miles north of the city near the village of Monument. As before, they owned the property, maintained the buildings, and cared for the horses, thus relieving JBS of menial tasks and daily responsibilities. Here, under the blue Colorado sky, he rode regularly—several hours each morning, six days a week—over the undulating range and through the pine-forested hills called the Black Forest. The ranch bore the JBS-approved name Flying Horse Ranch.

Some years later the Flints, again with JBS's financial backing, purchased for $180,000 from Edward B. Maclean, a beautiful 4,500-acre ranch closer to Colorado Springs. The Maclean ranch, with its spectacular view of Pike's Peak, included a commodious ranch house, a stone patio, stable, corrals, and outbuildings. Most of the structures, especially the house, reflected a Spanish style of architecture—pink stucco and adobe, balconies, metal grillwork, and tile. JBS nostalgically called this American version of

JBS on the trail with Rancheros Visitadores in California (1941)

JBS and friends at Salinas Rodeo (1942)

*Pike's Peak Avenue in Colorado Springs:
JBS's office on left and Antler's Hotel at center*

Dick Spencer, Editor and Publisher of
The Western Horseman *(1950)*

The Western Horseman *offices and personnel (1960)*

JBS in semi-western attire (1961)

his Hertfordshire estate Highfield West. His cosmopolitan and eclectic tastes were evident throughout the house. There was an English dining room with murals depicting a fox hunt and a fireplace framed by wood paneling, a French kitchen with an open hearth fireplace and beamed ceilings, a breakfast alcove furnished in Georgian decor, a large wine room with a corner bar and an indoor shuffleboard court, a recreation room with a piano and a billiard table, a large American-style living room (called the main lounge) with an Oriental corner, and of course a trophy room filled with mementos and photographs portraying polo matches, fox hunts, and races of years gone by. Scattered throughout the house were equine representations in every conceivable form — paintings, prints, china glazings, figurines, tapestries, murals, and statuettes — witnessing that the Flints and JBS were horse fanciers of the first order.

Their horses frequently took prizes, as in 1944 when a Palomino filly named Flying Amber, trained by Florence Flint, placed first in its class and was named grand champion at the National Western Stock Show in Denver. The following years Flying Boy and Flying Pilot, both owned and trained by JBS, won first prizes at the Colorado Springs Horse Show. Both at Flying Horse Ranch and at Highfield West, the Snow-Flint team bred high quality horses of various types — thoroughbred racers, quarter horses, and polo ponies. Beryl Eaton wrote in 1956, "Florence Flint told me this morning they have so many new colts at the ranch they've lost count — both thoroughbreds and quarter horses. Their stables are fabulous, and the house is one of the showplaces in this area."

Highfield West and its high quality horses won the acclaim of horse lovers in Colorado, from many of whom JBS received congratulatory mail. One youthful admirer from a nearby ranch wrote:

> Dear Mr. Snow,
> You know that beautiful palimino of yours. Well I wanted to know if we could feed him sugar. Because

every day I feed him bunches of grass. But, boy he's so beautiful and hansom. I sure say one thing, you sure do take care of him.

>Yours truly,
>William Xavier Barron (Age 9)
>R.R.3 Black Forest, Colo. Springs
>Colorado
>Phone No. 495-2751

P.S. That horse is the most beautiful horse in the world & everytime I feed him bunches of grass, and walk away he always kicks the fence with his hoof because he wants more.

Billy's request was honored, and several years later his father, Arch Barron, bought Highfield West as a family residence.

JBS's passion for horses and his business acumen coalesced when he purchased *The Western Horseman*, a magazine that stressed Western horse stock in its editorial policy and included cartoons, feature articles, and advertising. It was founded in 1936 by Mr. and Mrs. Paul Albert of Lafayette, California, and had a circulation of 9,000 in 1942 at the time of Mr. Albert's death. Upon purchasing the magazine from Mrs. Albert in 1943 for an undisclosed price, JBS moved the editorial and business offices from Lafayette to Reno, Nevada, and named Graham M. Dean, a friend of Merritt Speidel, as editor and publisher. At first the newly acquired magazine was put together by newsmen associated with the Speidel-owned newspapers in Reno. Though the magazine's editorial policy changed little for several years, gradually the new owner, whose identity long remained a secret, made changes in its scope and nature.

In 1948, at the direction of the silent owner, *The Western Horseman* was moved to Colorado Springs and the following year into its present offices, at that time a new, modern Spanish-style structure on the north side of the city. It also acquired a new general manager, Don Flint. This move signaled a policy change. Hitherto the magazine had been regional, limited to the West in scope and appeal; henceforth it would become national and, hopefully, the nation's number one horse magazine. The appointment of Richard Spencer as editor to implement the new policy proved to be a stroke of genius. The youngish, pipe-smoking Texan-Indian was an authentic child of the West, a lover of horses and horse-related activities, a cartoonist, and an outdoor enthusiast. He soon gave the magazine a new look and broader horizons. He changed the cover and format, enlarged the article and advertising space, increased the price, broadened the appeal, and more than doubled the circulation, from 50,000 in 1950 to 105,000 in 1970. At the time of Spencer's death in 1989, the circulation was about 190,000.

JBS took greater personal interest in *The Western Horseman* than in his other publishing ventures and felt much pride in its successes. He eagerly awaited the day each month that Rod Koht, the circulation manager, brought him the new issue. Gradually he permitted his name to be associated with the magazine and finally to appear on the masthead as chairman of the board. In 1961 he allowed Dick Spencer to feature him in a short illustrated article commemorating the twenty-fifth anniversary of the publication. Except, however, for an occasional suggestion, he followed a hands-off policy regarding the details of publication. Though he presided at board meetings and gave financial advice when needed, he remained in the background.

Dick Spencer fully realized the wisdom of JBS's managerial philosophy when he wrote in 1961:

> The more successful enterprises in the country are usually backed by men of either an abiding faith or an active interest—success may very often be the combination of faith and interest. John Ben Snow of Colorado Springs is a successful businessman and an avid horseman who had played a vital role in *The Western Horseman*, yet has remained in the background.

Similarly, twelve years later this eulogy written by Spencer in *The Western Horseman* underscored the same theme:

> JBS was a very successful businessman, in several different ventures; but we all felt that *The Western Horseman* merited his most special pride. Yet he was always in the background, and always let it run on a free rein. Decisions were always left to the active staff. He would tell us what he liked, and what he didn't like, but not once did he issue a "do this" or a "don't do that."

This free-rein approach to business ventures — a lesson he learned from the horse — proved to be the key to JBS's success.

As a horseman, however, JBS did not readily surrender his reins. After the Flints sold Highfield West in 1965 and moved to California, he arranged to ride at the small ranch of Glen Scribner, located a short distance from Highfield West. There he rode six days a week, sometimes with Scribner or Doc Eaton, Beryl Eaton's brother, often by himself, into his eighty-third year. However, in 1966 one of his horses bolted and threw him to the ground. Beryl Eaton reported:

> Fortunately no bones were broken but his bruises have been very, very painful, and he has been in the hospital since the day of the accident. He has been a wonderful patient and much interested in the hospital routines, this being his first experience.... Of course his doctor has x-rayed him from stem to stern and he is making all sorts of examinations, now that he has a captive patient.

When released a week later, JBS picked up the reins and continued his routine. But in February 1967 a second accident again sent him to the hospital for treatment of bruises and tests. Shortly after this incident he was forbidden by his physician, Dr. Robert Smith, ever to ride again, and he reluctantly ceased.

Even then the ever resourceful horseman secured his daily exercise by means of a mechanical horse. He had ridden electric horses on shipboard when crossing the Atlantic and

JBS mounted at Colorado Springs ranch (1958)

at the New York Athletic Club. Thus he arranged to have the same three-speed mechanical horse he had once given to Merritt Speidel shipped from Palo Alto to Colorado Springs and installed in the open basement of the Scribner ranch. There he affixed it to the floor, fitted it with one of his well-worn saddles, and surrounded it with artificial turf. Daily he would appear at exactly 8:30 a.m. at the Scribner ranch in his Rolls convertible, mount his steed, ride for the self-prescribed number of minutes, walk in the nearby woods, shower, then return to the Springs for lunch at the El Paso Club and an afternoon in the office. He continued this remarkable routine until shortly before his death in his ninetieth year.

VII

Chairman of the Board

JBS could without doubt be considered a success prior to his return to the States. He was a top corporate executive — one of five directors — in a large and expanding multinational corporation. He had an international reputation as the owner and breeder of winning racehorses. Yet success is relative, especially to those with high aspirations and ambitions. Though his horses won many of England's renowned races and placed in the Grand National, JBS failed to achieve a much-coveted first at Aintree. Similarly he never became chairman of the board of directors of F. W. Woolworth Ltd., a prize he wanted and probably deserved. Upon his return to America, especially after the sale of Highfield, he abandoned his hope of winning a Grand National or a Kentucky Derby. Instead he focused his aspirations on the attainment of success as a newspaper financier and executive.

As the silent partner of Merritt Speidel, JBS put up large amounts of cash for the purchase of several newspapers both before and after his return. With each purchase he became chairman of the board of each newspaper company, while Speidel assumed the title of president. By 1950 JBS served as chairman for eight newspaper companies, one radio station, and one periodical, *The Western Horseman*. However, he assumed a nondirective role in these Speidel affiliates and rarely concerned himself with local matters. Instead he devoted his time and energies to Speidel Newspapers, Inc. (SNI), the hub organization, of which he was also chairman of the board. As early as 1937 Speidel had stated, "When the organization goes over with a bang, I hope I can bring you out in the limelight where you belong, as chairman of the board of directors-in-chief." In response to Speidel's proddings, JBS did join several organizations, such as the San Francisco Press Club and Rotary, and showed some interest in the Masonic Order, but he continued to prefer obscurity to the limelight.

Despite this preference for anonymity, JBS supplied most of the capital for the purchase of additional newspapers and improvements. In 1939, after the outbreak of World War II, he had provided cash for the purchase of Reno Newspapers, Incorporated, which published two dailies—one Democratic and one Republican. Two years later he put up money for the purchase of two dailies in Poughkeepsie, New York, thus giving Speidel Newspapers a distinct advantage over its rivals. Because of the shortage of trained personnel and of newsprint, the Snow-Speidel team did not buy its next paper until after the war's end, when in 1948 they purchased Visalia Newspapers, Incorporated, for $100,000 and named as publisher Speidel's oldest son, Robert.

During these formative years of SNI, Silent Snow also supplied several hundred thousand dollars for improving the older plants in the expanding chain of newspapers. In 1937 he had provided money for the improvement of the *Iowa Press-Citizen* building in Iowa City and subsequently financed improvements in Salinas and Fort Collins. Between 1939 and 1941 he invested heavily in the Poughkeepsie "newspaper cathedral," an imposing structure near the center of the city that tourists sometimes confuse with a church because of its spire and design. The Snow-Speidel team firmly believed in providing each plant with the best possible working conditions—even air conditioning in a northern climate—and the most modern printing equipment. A pleasant plant was part of the Snow-Speidel creed.

By 1950 JBS virtually owned Speidel Newspapers, Inc., yet the extent of his proprietary interest remained obscure because of his unique method of financing. Not once had he personally negotiated a purchase or revealed the source of funds for capital improvements. In each case he loaned the necessary funds to his partner at one or two percent interest, and Speidel assumed the risk and responsibility for the investments. In 1950, when these loans totaled $2,000,000, they were consolidated into a single note with the interest slightly more than $20,000 a year. These financial intricacies remained hidden to all but a few in the inner circle of SNI. Some perceptive personnel in the affiliates as well as shrewd outsiders no doubt correctly perceived the Snow-Speidel relationship, but to the general public the Speidel company, like many other newspaper chains, was a family dominated concern.

In May 1937 when the new *Press-Citizen* buildings were dedicated, JBS appeared in Iowa City and attended the ceremonies along with his partner and other Speidel officers. Four years later he traveled by train from Palo Alto to Chillicothe, Ohio, to participate in a Speidel-sponsored event. To celebrate the opening of a new plant and to commemorate the 141st birthday of the *Chillicothe Gazette*, Merritt Speidel played host to "a galaxy of notables of the Fourth Estate." In his dedicatory address Governor John W. Bricker, the featured speaker, welcomed the return of Speidel to Ohio, lauded his publishing achievements, and reminded the audience that "freedom of the press has been sacredly preserved by the vigilance of newspaper men."

In a congratulatory letter, President Franklin D. Roosevelt wrote, "Now, as in the days when the Chillicothe newspapers were established, we as a free people need a free press as one of the sure guarantees of our democratic way of life." Similarly Governor Bricker noted, "Your papers have played a great part in the building of the Commonwealth of Ohio." After the dedicatory banquet at the Chillicothe Country Club, JBS permitted himself to be photographed and briefly interviewed. The photograph, later appearing in a local newspaper, showed Snow and Speidel along with a local news commentator. The caption listed Speidel as president of Chillicothe Newspapers, Incorporated, and Snow as "an associate of Mr. Speidel and director of Speidel Newspapers, Inc."

Several years later an anti-Speidel competitor, the *Poughkeepsie Square Dealer*, discussed the Snow-Speidel tie in a short front-page story. The buyer-publisher of the *Poughkeepsie New Yorker* was Merritt Speidel, so the account went, but "Mr. Speidel's backer and partner is John Ben Snow, multi-millionaire who lives in the West." Additional biographical facts about Speidel were for the most part accurate, but the biographical sketch of JBS was filled with errors. Thereafter, in the interest of accuracy, Snow "went public" in most matters relating to Speidel and SNI.

In 1952 JBS made journalism history by surrendering his paramount interest in and voting control of SNI. The purpose of the change was, in his words, "to place and assure perpetuation of the ownership and control of the newspapers in the Speidel group in hands of those producers actively engaged in management." Though Snow originated the idea, Harry Bunker worked out the complicated details of the new arrangement. To effect the plan, JBS exchanged his common stock, then valued at $4,500,000, and voting control for nonvoting preferred stock yielding low dividends. The common voting stock was then purchasable by the management of the individual newspapaers and by SNI executives, who could hold it as long as they were actively associated with the organization. At the end of his association with SNI, the shareholder was obliged to sell all shares to his successor or others still active in the organization. Also no shareholder could hold more than seven percent of the total shares. These changes resulted in a diffusion of financial and voting control and in a dilution of the influence of the Speidel family in the organization.

JBS's selflessly motivated reforms were featured in the 21 June 1952 issue of *Editor and Publisher*. The article, entitled "Snow Transfers Control to Speidel Executives," included a picture and an accurate biographical sketch of JBS along with an explanation of the transfer plan. It is significant to note the role reversal: Snow dominated the news story; Speidel figured in only one short paragraph. "Mr. Snow's plan is unparalleled in modern journalistic history," Speidel himself wrote. "It is another one of the many really great things accomplished through the years that had reflected the real greatness of the chairman of our board of directors and beloved friend—John Ben Snow." The plan, according to *Editor and Publisher*, represented a "healthy trend" in the publishing business.

Although no additional newspapers were acquired in the years between 1947 and 1963, significant changes took place in SNI. In May 1956 at the age of seventy-seven, Merritt Speidel stepped aside as president and was succeeded by Harry S. Bunker. That same year the individual newspapers and the central service organization in the Speidel group were consolidated into a single, more efficient organization. Its legal status changed in 1958, when SNI surrendered its Iowa charter and was reorganized as a Delaware corporation with 1,500,000 shares of common stock. The individual newspapers and their shareholders surrendered their affiliate status and became subsidiary companies, thereby allowing all shareholders to benefit from the consolidated profits of SNI and continue to share in the profits of the individual news companies.

These structural changes heralded the second period of expansion in SNI history. Between 1963 and 1969 three new papers were added to the Speidel chain. In February 1963 the *Argus-Leader* of Sioux Falls, South Dakota, with a circulation of fifty thousand, was purchased during Harry Bunker's presidency. Three years later, during the tenure of Charles Stout, the Fremont, Nebraska *Tribune* became part of the Speidel group. In 1969 President Jack Liechty purchased the *Stockton* (California) *Record*, the largest newspaper in terms of circulation and revenue.

Though JBS did not provide the capital for these purchases, he gave financial advice and provided business contacts. For example, he recommended that the purchases be financed through a secured loan from the Irving Trust Company rather than through the use of accumulated profits or by going public. Through his contacts with George A. Murphy, then chairman of the board of Irving Trust, SNI borrowed the funds needed to buy the three papers. These interlocking connections were evident in a congratulatory letter which JBS received from Murphy in February 1963:

> Dear John,
>
> I know how pleased and proud you must be at the addition of the Argus-Leader of Sioux Falls to the Speidel Newspapers group. This is in keeping with the sound tradition of growth and quality which always characterized your guidance of Speidel Newspapers and we congratulate you and Harry and your associates on this fine development. Naturally, we are happy with the part which Irving Trust was able to play in the financing arrangements. Warm personal regards,
>
> Sincerely,
>
> George

When SNI went public, as it did in the fall of 1972, Irving Trust handled the financial side of the transaction. Thus the preferred bank of F. W. Woolworth, with JBS as the connecting link, now became the creditor of Speidel Newspapers, Inc.

* * *

JBS's role in the Speidel organization was far removed from the din of the pressroom. He devoted little time to news gathering or to the mechanical aspects of publishing; he took some interest in physical makeup and editorial writing but rendered only personal opinion, not professional advice. Although he assumed a publisher's point of view in matters relating to national politics, controversial local issues, and labor relations, he refused to impose his ideas or prejudices on a particular newspaper, in contrast to many other newspaper magnates. Instead he limited his attention to the big questions. With Speidel he hoped to recruit and retain able, hard-working, innovative people, to

*JBS in Speidel Newspapers Office
in Colorado Springs, Colorado (1963)*

JBS and Speidel Newspapers associates at banquet in Colorado Springs

instill in them the tenets of the Speidel creed, to inspire them to maintain the highest standards of journalism, and to assist them in their personal and organizational goals. The function of the chairman of the board, as JBS viewed his role, was to inspire, encourage, exemplify, advise, motivate, look ahead, and take the long view.

The Snow-Speidel business creed emphasized opportunity. Early in his life JBS had been exposed to the teachings of John D. Rockefeller, Jr.:

> Every right implies a responsibility,
> Every opportunity, an obligation.

Successful business leaders should seek out and recruit able and industrious young men and offer them an opportunity to prove themselves. They in turn had the obligation to work for the good of the organization and advance its mission. Thus, just as he had benefited from the early opportunity offered by Fred Woolworth, so did JBS incorporate that philosophy in his creed so that it permeated the Speidel Newspaper organization. The publication of newspapers involved more than the mere making of profits; it also served moral and social purposes. Newspapers should be "clean," stimulating, uplifting, and responsive to community needs and ideals. "Give your community the best and most progressive newspaper you can publish," Speidel advocated. "Countenance only clean journalism. Be politically independent. Avoid racial and religious bias. Dedicate your newspapers to the highest ideals of the community." More concretely the Snow-Speidel team championed such causes as honest government, community libraries, recreational facilities, public health, good roads, and ethical conduct in business. The focus of the news reported was local rather than national, and the editorials encouraged and praised. JBS firmly believed in this journalistic creed and used the authority of his office to disseminate it.

In his position as chairman, JBS presided over the board meetings. His formal training in parliamentary procedure at the Academy plus his countless board meetings at Woolworth's enabled him to do this with considerable ease. He knew when to speak and when to pound the gavel. In 1958, in recognition both of his presiding role and of his seventy-fifth birthday he was presented with a gavel made from a maple tree located near the Snow homestead in Pulaski. Speidel associates conceived the idea; Frances Wart, the daughter of Orimell Olmstead, secured the wood; Gerald Frazer, a Pulaski woodworker, contributed his skill at the lathe; and Tiffany's of New York City supplied the gold-plated inscription that read:

>JOHN BEN SNOW
>CHAIRMAN OF THE BOARD
>SPEIDEL NEWSPAPERS INC.
>JUNE 16, 1958

It became one of JBS's most treasured possessions.

His annual speeches, more properly pep-talks, were invariably short, crisp, and to the point and were frequently interlaced with pithy epigrams:

> He that thinketh by the inch
> and speaketh by the yard
> should be kicketh by the foot.

> or

> If adversity comes, BAT IT DOWN!

Usually he provided a touch of humor, either by inflection or a smile, and generally sought to encourage, to motivate, to reach out for the reality of the dream.

As chairman of the board, he at times felt compelled to educate publishers and editors on the fundamentals of journalism. Sometimes his pep-talks assumed a didactic flavor, as the following homily on "Accuracy" demonstrates:

> We have three rules: accuracy, ACCURACY, *ACCURACY*:
>
> BE PRECISE. Tell exactly what happened without embellishment. A minor disturbance is not a riot.
>
> CREDIBILITY. Source of information most important. Keep emotions under control. Check and double check; tell it as it is.

DAMAGE. AP quoted unqualified source that damage in Detroit "exceeds $1 billion." Investigation showed it to be $40 to $45 million.

PERSPECTIVE. Keep story in focus. A crowd broken up in 15 minutes should not be phrased "crowds roamed the streets through the night."

BACKGROUND. All disputes have a history and we should know enough about the town to say what it is.

STAFFING. Get men to the scene at the first hint of trouble. Keep in touch with the desk . . .

We will not gloss over the facts. Our reporting and writing should be reasonable, understandable, logical and orderly.

JBS's written communications reflected the same passion for precision and economy. He detested pedantry and verbosity. Rarely did he send a memo to SNI personnel; rarely did he write a letter. Rather his principal method of communication, aside from the telephone, was the Western Union yellow printed form. However, except when urgency demanded otherwise, he had his secretary type the message on the form, enclose it in an envelope, and send it by way of the U.S. Postal Service. Typical of this favorite method of communication is the following "Snowgram" addressed to his New York attorney:

Plan arrive N.Y. March 19.
Trustees met March 14, 1960.
Hope can hold similar meeting!
Paul should join us this year!

Am I correct Foundation gifts amount to $57,000?
If so, we are well over the $45,000 income.

Will renew Irving note for $400,000 March 8.
Will have plenty cash balance to buy 2550 T shares @ $86.

Has Foundation sufficient cash to take advantage of T offer and also add 90 shares to total 300?

This abbreviated form of message, if nothing else, served to cut down on stationery and secretarial costs.

JBS's penchant for brevity and his depersonalized stationery were a vestige of his years with Woolworth Ltd. When in England, his communications with relatives and friends had been by cablegrams. When a buyer, he had sent his orders and messages by means of national or international telegram. Thus did the earlier routine practice become the idiosyncratic trademark of the chairman of the board.

JBS conceived it his duty as chairman of the board to be well-informed on many subjects. His sources of information were many: radio, television, but primarily the printed word. He generally devoted four to six hours a day to reading, even after his eyesight began to fail and he was forced to use a magnifying glass and to subscribe to the large-print edition of the *New York Times*. A preference for brevity also characterized his reading habits. In later years he rarely read a full-length book, much preferring abridged reading material. He enjoyed *Life*, *The London Illustrated News*, and the humor in *Punch*. For daily news he relied heavily upon local papers, television commentators, and the capsulized news items on the front page of the *Wall Street Journal*. He read *Time* and *Newsweek* thoroughly each week. Each month he read many magazines, several newsletters dealing with finance, and reports from SNI and other corporations in which he had investments. *Reader's Digest* was his favorite light reading; rarely was he without the latest issue in his pocket or at least an article torn from it. Occasionally he read the abridged versions of best-sellers, also published by *Reader's Digest*. The fact that the publishers of the *Digest* were upstate New Yorkers merely added to his pleasure.

For inspirational reading JBS turned to the Bible, copies of which were to be found beside his bed and on his office desk. Dog-eared pages reflected a preference for the words and deeds of Jesus, especially those in the Sermon on the Mount. Scattered slips of paper tucked in books or file folders give a glimpse of the inner man. One note card contains a self-composed admonition written in indelible pencil:

> Lord, fill my mouth with worthwhile stuff,
> And nudge me when I've said enough!

On another he jotted:

> Today's *avant*
> is
> Tomorrow's *passé*.

On a colorful greeting card that depicted two galloping horses, each with a broken halter and moving in a different direction, JBS inscribed in blue pencil the word FREEDOM!

As chairman of the board, John Ben Snow preached and practiced the old-style virtues of honesty, integrity, discipline, self-reliance, charity, and hard work, values shared by Speidel, and together they sought subordinates with similar views and commitments. They recruited experienced personnel, tested men who began at the bottom and worked their way to the top. At the same time they appreciated the value of a college or university education. Because he had close ties with several educators in the School of Journalism, Merritt Speidel staffed many positions with graduates of the University of Iowa, especially those who had been associated with the campus newspaper, thus producing an "Iowa Syndrome" in SNI.

JBS not only supported this personnel policy; he continued it after his partner's retirement. Hence Speidel's successors were Harry S. Bunker in 1956, Charles H. Stout in 1964, and Jack Leichty in 1969. These presidents of SNI, all Iowans, had been associated with the *Iowa City Press-Citizen*; most of them had worked on the *Daily Iowan*, the student newspaper at the University. All began at the bottom and had years of experience in newspaper publishing, on either the news or the business end, before becoming president. They brought into the organization William T. Hagebroeck, Edwin B. Green, Kenneth E. Green, and Johanna Nelson, all associated with the *Daily Iowan* and the *Press-Citizen*, plus many others. Only the last president, Rollan Melton, did not enter SNI during the tenure of Speidel. However, after securing a journalism degree from the

University of Nevada, he began his meteoric career at the bottom, like Snow and Speidel, and moved up from reporter to editor and then publisher before succeeding Liechty in 1972 at the age of forty.

* * *

In 1953, after the reorganization plan achieved national acclaim, a laudatory editorial featuring JBS appeared in *SNI Home News*, the house organ of Speidel Newspapers. The author of the tribute, Merritt Speidel, first apologized for the inadequacy of words:

> Any editorial or personal appraisal of Mr. Snow's life, character and accomplishments would fall short of doing him full justice. It would take a large volume to approach adequacy, and then with the depth of feeling of affection and admiration of those who knew him so well, it would be difficult to restrain oneself from emotional enthusiasm.

Nevertheless, wrote Speidel, it was possible to eulogize JBS in both negative and positive terms:

> It is a pleasure to write something of the negative side of Mr. Snow's character. Nobody in this country, nor in England, to my knowledge, has ever been able to say that he has ever done anything mean, low, petty, shabby or vulgar, nor have any of his acts of life ever been motivated by any ignoble or ulterior purposes. It's a fine thing sometimes to be known by what we are not, as well as by what we are. Because of his unimpeachable character, Mr. Snow is blessed both ways.

Speidel briefly recounted his early ties with JBS:

> Having been associated with him in the church, and having been with him in our home towns in New York State, and having been associated with him in various other sections of New York, California, in England and elsewhere, and now in Colorado, I have seen him operate in business, in social and other phases of life—always with the true Christian spirit of brotherly love,

> and always with the highest sense of honor, integrity and consideration for the rights of others. His clean, wholesome, unblemished life, his kindly disposition, his innate love and patriotism for his native United States are all combined in the connotations of what a real American should be.

JBS's greatness and goodness, at least in Speidel's estimation, stemmed from his sterling character, which in turn came from "natural endowment" and "the atmosphere of a true home and Godly parentage."

> In him you see the touch of a mother's molding power and a strong and guiding hand of a religious father. In the phraseology of the world, it may be said he comes from religious stock. He has been trained on the principle that "Whatsoever a man soweth, that shall he also reap."

Snow was not a "Sunday Christian" in Speidel's eyes. Rather he lived by religious principles seven days a week.

> Despite the cynical philosophy toward business and businessmen, to some degree in this country as well as elsewhere in the world, it is not straining a metaphor to say that Mr. Snow's honest and honorable business methods and his exemplary personal life have run parallel. Always he has been the honest, the forthright, the true Christian businessman, deeply concerned with the rights and problems of his fellow men. He has been as meticulous and as honest in his business affairs as he has in his personal living.

These words of praise did not, however, forestall the inevitable eclipse of Merritt Speidel in the organization he had conceived, founded, and nurtured. The aforementioned changes in structure and personnel diluted his personal influence and control in the corporation that bore his name, as well as the role of his family in the future of SNI. In 1956, when Speidel retired, he first resigned from the subsidiary companies he had presided over for many years, then from the parent corporation, SNI, and surrendered his shares according to the terms of the reorganization plan. So ended the long and successful business venture between Snow and Speidel. The two men continued, however, to keep in touch. Speidel communicated through long, handwritten letters filled with nostalgic reminiscences and flowery tributes; Snow responded by telegram or postal card. Periodically they chatted with each other on the telephone.

Even after Speidel's death in 1960, JBS received a message from his onetime friend, for he wrote in his last will and testament:

> I would not desire to close this codicil without a final greeting to Mr. John Ben Snow . . . a valued friend of more than a half century. By conscientious efforts and most difficult, hard work, buttressed by an unblemished character, he had acquired a competence beyond consideration of monetary gifts. I am therefore willing to him the same depth of love and supreme happiness that he has brought into my life for more than half a century of unblemished friendship, with the reverent prayers that he will enjoy vibrant health and happiness so long as he shall live, and then join me in facing Eternity.

For twelve more years, until his own death, Snow continued to serve as chairman of the board. He discontinued his periodic train trips to New York City, eventually eliminating all travel from his schedule, and reluctantly assumed a more sedentary existence. He did, however, attend those SNI meetings held in Colorado Springs and presided over the annual meetings of SNI, the Snow Foundation, and *The Western Horseman*. But in reality he became an honorary chief executive.

Most of JBS's personal associations were with members of what he termed his "Speidel family," persons in the SNI organization, especially those living in Colorado Springs: Harry and Laureda Bunker, Chick and Betty Stout, Beryl Eaton and her brother Doc Eaton, Don and Florence Flint, as well as Dorothy Vandenberg and others who worked in the central office. Some members of JBS's Speidel family migrated to Reno in 1964 as a result of the board's decision to move the central office there, a decision JBS reluctantly agreed to, but the nucleus remained in Colorado Springs. The Bunkers and Flints both retired there. Beryl Eaton continued as personal secretary to both Harry Bunker and JBS until she was succeeded, upon her retirement in 1970, by Dorothy Vandenberg. Doc Eaton remained JBS's close companion until his death in 1970. During his last years JBS became more and more dependent upon these members of his Speidel family for fellowship, advice, assistance, and consolation.

JBS confided chiefly in Harry Bunker. Their long-standing mutual respect and understanding, resulting from Bunker's close relationship with both Snow and Speidel, evolved into a confiding friendship between 1956 and 1966. Together JBS and Bunker rode the range; together they talked shop, meaning newspaper finance and business in general; together they planned philanthropic projects. Frequently Harry lunched with Snow at the El Paso Club, and occasionally JBS consented to spend a Christmas or Thanksgiving with the Bunkers. No one took Harry Bunker's place after his death from cancer in 1966. No one could.

Though not particularly past-conscious, JBS kept up his ties with Pulaski in several ways. He corresponded sporadically with Orimell Olmstead and regularly with his daughter, Frances Wart, especially after she moved into the Snow homestead in 1956. Periodically he chatted by telephone with Mrs. Hugh Barclay, the daughter of the late Harry Moody. Eventually through his cousin Ralph Snow, who became the Snow family almoner in 1958, JBS bestowed upon the village of his birth hundreds of thousands of dollars. His hopes, springing from deep sentiments, focused on the betterment of the community.

During his last years JBS became more introspective and philosophical about life and death. A short poem entitled "After Seventy," found among his last effects, aptly reflects his mood:

> Pamper the body
> Prod the soul.
> Accept limitations
> But play a role.
> Withdraw from the front
> But stay in the fight.
> Avoid isolation—
> Keep in sight.
> Beware reminiscing
> Except to a child.
> To forgetting proper names
> Be reconciled . . .
> Refrain from loquacity
> Be crisp and concise.
> And regard self-pity
> As a cardinal vice.

These lines, though not written by JBS, reflect his attitude toward life during his last years.

Though he did not indulge in self-pity, he did pamper his body during the final decade of his long life. He paid close attention to his diet; he cut down his consumption of sauterne, his favorite wine; he smoked fewer cigars; he forsook all pastries and most candies. He also arranged for his personal physician, Dr. Robert Smith, to visit him regularly—first monthly, then weekly, finally semiweekly—for physical checkups and advice. Generally JBS adhered to the advice of "Dr. Bob," for whom he had great respect and affection, but sometimes he reversed roles and gave Dr. Bob his prescription for longevity. Ever conscious of his short, and shrinking stature, he made every effort to walk erect and never ceased to take pride in his sturdy frame, his crunching handshake, his active mind, and his formula for longevity. He hated to admit illness; he disliked nurses; he deplored hospitals. He much preferred to "stay in the fight" and to die with riding boots on.

JBS rarely talked about death; nevertheless, he possessed a healthy attitude toward it. He did not welcome death as a martyr or a terminally ill patient might, nor did he fear dying. He accepted the reality and inevitability of death as

Formal portrait of JBS (1973)

the fate of all human beings. He prepared himself for that reality psychologically and practically by means of a last will and testament. At the same time he believed in life after death, subscribing to the traditional Christian view regarding immortality. For all mankind there was hope that the soul lived on after death. For those who loved God and followed the teachings of Christ, there was the promise of everlasting life. There also existed a close connection between the here and the hereafter in JBS's view, and that relationship was best expressed in the words of Jesus:

> Whatsoever a man soweth,
> that shall he also reap.

VIII

The Philanthropist

JBS was not a great man in the final analysis; rather he was a good man. He was not perfect, to be sure, for he had shortcomings and frailties. He was always demanding and proud, sometimes gruff and short-tempered. Nevertheless, he possessed what the Greeks termed *virtu* and what Christian theologians call goodness: he was high-minded, upright, tolerant, liberal, forgiving, and above all, generous with his wealth and worldly possessions.

JBS's selfless generosity — a generosity of deeds, not empty words — sprang from his Christian home and early religious training. His liberal attitude toward money and material possessions was reinforced by association with the Rockefellers and with Merritt Speidel and by continuous reading of the Bible, especially the New Testament. The dog-eared pages and marked passages of his Bibles provide clues to his motivation. The following passage from the Sermon on the Mount stands out:

> Take heed that ye do not your alms before men, to be seen of them: otherwise ye have no reward of your Father which is in heaven. Therefore when thou doest thine alms, do not sound a trumpet before thee . . . But when thou doest alms, let not thy left hand know what thy right hand doeth.

The spirit of true generosity rather than the gift was all-important, as this poem, found among JBS's papers after his death, makes clear:

> Tis not the weight of jewel or plate
> Or the fondle of silk or fur;
> Tis the spirit in which the gift is rich
> As the gifts of the wise ones were.

JBS was a giver of countless gifts. He received satisfaction from giving. He gave freely, not grudgingly, and in so doing demonstrated his love of man and God. On the other hand, he was not a self-denying ascetic. He believed that the world was good, not evil, and that man was expected to work hard and enjoy the fruits of his labors. And if the hard-working man accumulated more than his needs required, he was expected to use the excess accumulation (capital) wisely, for man was in fact a steward of God.

JBS combined these Protestant beliefs — beliefs upheld by Andrew Carnegie and John D. Rockefeller — with his own views on the corruptibility of riches. Wealth, like power, tends to corrupt; or to quote the apostle Paul, "The love of money is the root of all evil." However, as he reminded this author on one particularly memorable occasion, money itself is neutral, neither good nor evil. Rather the *love of money* is evil.

JBS enjoyed life, he especially enjoyed making money as a competitive game of wits, but money remained the means, not the end. The fate of those money-makers who lived for money alone was doubtful at best, as the following reminder found in his desk drawer illustrates:

> Nine Outstanding Kings of Finance — Learned the Art of Making Money — Not the Art of LIVING
>
> *C.* Schwab — Steel — Last 5 yrs. on borrowed money.
> *R.* Whitney — President Stock Exchange — Sing Sing.
> *A.* Cutten — Wheat Jockey — Died abroad insolvent.
> *S.* Insull — Utilities — Died a foreign fugitive.
> *H.* Hopson — Gas and Oil — Insane.
> *J.* Livermore — Wall Street Bear — Suicide.
> *A.* Fall — President's Cabinet — Prison — Home to die.
> *I.* Kreuger — Monopolist — Suicide.
> *L.* Fraser — Pres. Bank Int. Settlement — Suicide.

These financiers perverted the use of money; they abused their trust; they reaped what they had sowed.

In contrast, the true steward regarded money as an instrument, a tool, not as the end of life itself; thus he was neither ascetic nor miser but a life-loving trustee. As such he worked assiduously, invested wisely, and gave generously.

* * *

From these wellsprings of Christian benevolence flowed an ever-widening stream of gifts. At times JBS gave cash, often securities, sometimes property and personal possessions. His vehicles were several, the beneficiaries many and varied. He occasionally gave in person but more often relied upon an intermediary — a friend, a personal representative, a financial institution, a charitable organization. Often he insisted upon anonymity. Always he gave quietly, inconspicuously, and genuinely.

As already noted, JBS bestowed gifts upon friends and associates throughout his adult life. As early as 1909 he gave Merritt Speidel money to purchase a newspaper. This was a gift, not a loan. Thirty years later he transferred to his partner-friend shares of securities valued at $1,000,000. He also gave thousands of securities to horse-loving friends and Woolworth associates in England. The gifts in these cases reflected the affection and gratitude of a shy and slow-speaking bachelor.

Squire Snow's munificence overflowed at Highfield. He provided food, drink, sporting equipment, horses, entertainment, and lodging for his horse-loving friends; even interested onlookers were welcome. Hospitality and conviviality went hand in hand at Highfield. For the domestic help and farm laborers, JBS assumed the role of Santa Claus. According to Geoffrey Head,

> Christmas Eve was a time of great excitement in the "Head" household. We waited for the message, which was always brought by old Mr. Brooks, for my father to call at the bungalow to have a drink with JB. We then

> had to wait for him to return bearing presents for us all from JB and Jeanne Grenier, and there always was plenty; in fact, I remember one year my father had to bring them back in a tea chest which was full.

His kind gestures toward the country folk—an attitude characteristic of the English squirearchy—acquired legendary qualities; he is still fondly remembered as Goose Green's Mr. Christmas.

The earliest records of JBS's contributions to charitable organizations dates back to 1928. In that year, though living in England, he made donations to the American Red Cross, the Iowa City Social Services League, and the Boy Scouts of America, one of his favorite charities. In effect, he gave away all the yearly dividends from his share of the *Iowa City Press-Citizen* to local causes, with his partner Speidel acting on his behalf. In subsequent years, instead of dispersing his share of the profits to several causes, he gave it to the Boy Scouts. Most of the money was used to build and improve a campground west of Iowa City. In 1937 he provided funds to erect a dining pavilion and meeting hall at the camp, insisting that this gift as well as the earlier ones be made anonymously.

This plea for anonymity persisted three years later when he donated $24,000 to the New York University chapter of Alpha Kappa Psi, a business fraternity. This gift, the first of its kind, sparked the establishment of the Alpha Kappa Psi Foundation. The money was used to underwrite scholarships and promote education in the area of business and finance.

The deep-rooted affection of JBS for his hometown and its people was shown in several ways. An avid reader of the *Pulaski Democrat*, he paid close attention to local news. His compassion was aroused whenever he read accounts of local fires, accidents, disasters, and deaths. Fully aware of the poverty of the villagers, especially during the Great Depression, he devised a long-distance method of benevolence. To many unfortunate victims of tragedy he mailed money—sometimes simply a five- or ten-dollar bill, sometimes larger amounts—but always anonymously. Fearing he would be discovered if the envelopes were postmarked London, he arranged for his banker in New York City to withdraw cash from his account and mail it from Manhattan. For years the identity of the Good Samaritan remained a mystery.

Similarly during the Depression (probably in 1933), the *Pulaski Democrat* was scheduled to be auctioned because of near bankruptcy. JBS, who was in the States at the time, provided the editor-publisher with enough funds ($10,000) to forestall bankruptcy and continue publication. The auction never took place. The Good Samaritan quickly vanished, demanding concealment of his name. Not long after this incident he also contributed $3,000 to the Pulaski Baptist Church and smaller amounts to the Congregational Church, the Boy Scouts, and the Girl Scouts.

Through the years, especially after his return to the States, JBS made regular contributions to religious organizations. He rarely attended church services and did not participate in other church-related activities, for institutional religion was not to his liking. Nevertheless, he was committed to meditation and prayer and to reading the Bible, devotional literature, and religious magazines. He supported the interdemoninational American Bible Society and several Protestant churches when there were special needs, for example, the Community Church of Palo Alto for a new electric organ and the Grace Episcopal Church of Colorado Springs.

More important than these sporadic gifts, JBS supported the Pulaski Baptist Church and Society throughout most of his adult life. He retained his membership there, even though residing thousands of miles away, and kept in touch with the several pastors and some members. While in England, especially after his mother's death, he gave to the church on a regular basis. Upon his return he established a special reserve fund to which he at first contributed $3,000 each year. From 1959 until his death, the Snow Foundation gave the church $5,000 each year.

JBS also gave money to his hometown church for special

needs, such as hymnals, a stained glass window, and in 1954 the electrification of the organ. The next year he provided the church with a Schulmerich carillon as a memorial to the Snow family. Here anonymity was impossible, since the bells were dedicated in a public ceremony and the newspaper ran a lead article soon after. "The bells are a gift to the church and the community," the *Pulaski Democrat* reported, "from John Ben Snow of Colorado, who has maintained a deep interest in the church." While observing that he had been a nonresident for many years, the article called him a "staunch supporter of his church" and noted, "He is following the aims and desires of his forefathers in 'keeping the bells ringing.'"

A few years later JBS presented the Snow homestead in Pulaski to the community. This property had been maintained by a local caretaker and occupied each summer by Anna Caldwell, an unmarried cousin, until her death in 1951. Thereafter Robert and Frances Wart lived there until Ralph and Mary Snow, JBS's cousins from Illinois, moved into the homestead in 1962. In July 1963, at Ralph Snow's suggestion, JBS donated the property to the Pulaski Public Library. It remained the village library until 1976, when that organization moved into the Snow Memorial Building, and is now occupied by the Pulaski Historical Society.

* * *

JBS's generosity toward his family demands special consideration. After his mother's death in 1916, he had almost no relatives bearing the Snow name aside from those cousins who lived in the Midwest. He did have a cousin on his mother's side of the family, Anna Caldwell, and several on his father's side: first cousins Grace Fenton and her sister Emily Fenton Hoyt, and the latter's daughters, Jessie and Sarah Hoyt. From 1916 to 1933 these women accepted JBS's invitation to summer at the Snow homestead.

In 1933 JBS rebuilt the house to accommodate Grace Fenton, a retired schoolteacher, but she died in White Plains before the house was completed. Thereafter his favorite cousin, Anna Caldwell, returned to Pulaski each summer, caring for the house and keeping in touch with JBS by mail throughout the years he was in England. Upon returning to the States in 1939, he gave Anna advice and financial assistance, including four thousand shares of Woolworth & Company Ltd., which she retained until her death, so that she could retire from her nursing position in Amsterdam, New York. JBS handled her funeral arrangements through his attorney, Talbot Malcolm, and the subsequent probate of her estate. He received the bulk of the estate, most of which he had given her, and in turn used it for the benefit of others, among them the Fentons of New York City.

Emily Fenton Hoyt had died three years earlier. Because JBS had felt deeply obligated to the Hoyt family, especially the daughters, ever since he had lived with them while attending NYU, he now assisted them financially. Both were retired and unmarried. Sarah, a former secretary, died in 1955; Jessie, a former schoolteacher, died ten years later. All of these cousins were buried in the Pulaski cemetery, some in the Snow plot.

Meanwhile JBS came in contact with his Snow cousins in the Midwest. In 1954 he was visited by Ralph and Mary Snow, who were vacationing in the Colorado Springs area. Ralph, then a dean at the Moody Bible Institute in Chicago, was the family genealogist and archivist. He had studied the history of the Snows and pieced together a family tree. He had known of JBS for several years and realized that they were cousins once removed, but he knew little beyond the facts recorded in JBS's *Who's Who* entry. The discovery of each other and their common ancestry was, in JBS's words, "an answer to a prayer." In 1962 he induced Ralph to leave the Moody Bible Institute and become his personal representative or almoner. He arranged for Ralph to move into the Snow homestead, which had been occupied by the Wart family for several years, and bestowed on him the family heirlooms, many from the mid-nineteenth century. He charged Ralph with the responsibility of initiating and overseeing philanthropic projects in upstate New York, particularly in Pulaski, and of helping his long-lost Snow cousins.

Through Ralph Snow—dubbed "the Big Snowflake" due to his portly frame—JBS disbursed hundreds of thousands of dollars. Through Ralph he made a general distribution of many thousands to his Snow cousins; he provided funds for the education of several college-bound Snows; he gave financial assistance to some in need. To insure the continuance of these activities, which gave him great satisfaction, JBS included in his will a testamentary trust designed to benefit the Snow family for several generations. He also brought Ralph into the Snow Foundation and placed him in charge of its numerous projects in upstate New York.

* * *

In 1948, after long discussions with Talbot Malcolm, JBS had established the Snow Foundation as a vehicle for his philanthropic activities. The organization, incorporated under New York State laws, called for an undesignated number of members, a five-man board of directors, and four officers—president, vice president, treasurer, and secretary. JBS was president until his death; Talbot Malcolm was executive vice president, succeeding JBS as president in 1973. The charter members included Harry Bunker and William Feick, friend and banker at the Irving Trust Company.

The initial capital, donated by JBS, amounted to $1,000 cash and several thousand shares of Woolworth common stock. Thereafter, each year for twenty-five years, he contributed additional funds, usually in the form of securities. (*See Table I, p. 150*) He never submitted a bill to the Foundation or received any money from it. By 1956 the assets of the Foundation totaled over $1,000,000. None of the directors received compensation. Since operating expenses were minimal, almost all of the income went into grants to educational, religious, or community causes.

The first grant was made to New York University in 1949.

For the next five years the directors disbursed all but $1,000 to JBS's alma mater, and over the years it has been the most regular recipient of funds from the Foundation. The actual amount of the grant increased steadily from $1,000 in 1949 to $10,000 in 1951 to $25,000 in 1957. Some years the grants went into the general fund; often they were earmarked for a specific purpose, especially scholarships; frequently they supplemented personal gifts made by JBS.

The largest single grant went to Syracuse University in 1965, when the Foundation provided $1,000,000 to endow journalism research in the Newhouse School of Communications. The income from the endowment was used to underwrite a research professorship known as the John Ben Snow Chair, undergraduate scholarships, and research assistantships, all with the intention of broadening the boundaries of knowledge in the field of newspaper journalism. The grant won the plaudits of both educators and newspaper executives. JBS replenished the capital resources of the Foundation, which as a result of this grant were depleted by nearly 50 percent, with generous contributions of additional securities.

Several other educational institutions benefited from Snow Foundation funds. From 1959 to 1968 Cornell University received annual grants varying from $1,000 to $10,000. JBS's favorite fraternity, Alpha Kappa Psi, received $1,000 in 1954, $35,000 in 1961, and $15,000 in 1962. In 1960 Phi Gamma Delta fraternity received $25,000. The Westminster Foundation of Cornell University was awarded smaller sums from 1953 to 1955.

Beginning in 1957 the Snow Foundation disbursed funds to the Pulaski Baptist Church. In 1957 and 1958 the amount was $3,000; since 1959 the grant has been $5,000 annually. The Scotia Baptist Church was granted $11,000 in 1963 for its building program, the Hudson Baptist Church $4,000 in 1965, and the Colosse Baptist Church $3,000 the same year. All of these gifts reflected the deep-seated gratitude of the donor toward the faith of his forebears.

Since 1964, especially after Ralph Snow became a member, the Foundation has steadily increased its contributions to projects in Pulaski, principally education, community improvement, and cultural advancement. Grants have been made to enhance and maintain the Pulaski Public Library, to improve the sanitary system, to provide much needed beautification for the cemetery, to purchase an organ for the high school, to provide better medical, hospital, and ambulance services, and to enhance the education of high school teachers. In addition, recurrent budget items have included annual grants to the Boy Scouts of America, to the Pulaski High School for John Ben Snow scholarships providing a college education for superior students, to Pulaski Academy for incentive awards to the highest achievers in each grade, and to high school students attending the summer Press Institute at Syracuse University.

Between 1962 and 1973, through the Foundation and personal giving, JBS contributed over $2,000,000 to various projects in central New York, including well over $600,000 to Pulaski. While the funds for these projects came from JBS's fortune, the ideas and overall planning, as well as post-grant supervision, must be credited to the ingenuity and labors of Ralph Snow. It was JBS's hope and intention that after his death the Foundation would continue this pattern of grants to Pulaski.

In addition to his annual contribution to the Foundation, JBS gave large amounts of cash and securities to his friends and favorite causes. Foremost was New York University. Beginning in 1952 he provided funds for the John Ben Snow Scholars at NYU's law school. The scholars, runners-up in the Root-Tilden competition, were a great source of satisfaction to him, for many of them distinguished themselves as lawyers and judges. He followed their careers with interest and kept track of them by means of pictures, letters, and a large scrapbook.

His deep-felt appreciation to business education also found expression in several large donations. Between 1962 and 1972 he participated in the building program of NYU's College of Business and Public Administration (the School of Commerce, when JBS attended) with gifts amounting to more than $350,000, all of which went into Tisch Hall. In addition, the college received $100,000 in 1972 to support undergraduate scholarships. The Graduate School of Business Administration also received $100,000 for similar purposes in 1971 and 1972.

Over the years contributions to the University (including the medical school) totaled more than $1,500,000. To this day the name of John Ben Snow is very much a living part of the NYU scene. There is the John Ben Snow Scholars program, the John Ben Snow Room at the Graduate School of Business Administration, the Snow Dining Room in Vanderbilt Hall (School of Law), the Snow Dining Room at the Medical Center, and in 1973 NYU's board of trustees named their newly completed meeting facility the John Ben Snow Memorial Room.

For these and numerous other acts of generosity JBS will be remembered, and his goodness will live on through the institutions he established or supported during his lifetime. To perpetuate his philanthropic ideals, he relied upon legal instruments, relatives, and friends. Through the Snow Foundation he hoped to benefit others, particularly upstate New Yorkers, in perpetuity. Through his will he established two testamentary trusts: (1) a family trust designed to benefit his "Snowflake" cousins, the descendants of Charles Snow, and (2) a charitable trust designed to assist those causes favored by JBS and others which were consistent with his principles.

JBS resisted the temptation to impose rigid guidelines on his trustees. He could have pinpointed certain organizations as special beneficiaries and in so doing perpetuated his favorite causes, but this he refused to do, for he believed that change is inherent in the nature of things and that flexibility is more desirable than rigidity. Since old needs give way to new, man must respond in like fashion. He entrusted the guardians of his fortune with the responsibility of using their best judgment and acting accordingly. Nevertheless, it is possible to distill from JBS's life certain guiding principles that motivated his philanthropy. His giving was people-oriented, for he preferred to invest in human beings, most specifically the young of America. He turned down several requests for funds to erect buildings. He resisted the temptation to contribute to animal-oriented causes, despite his love for animals, especially horses. Instead he preferred educational and religious causes, particularly those dedicated to character building, high moral standards, quality performance, and community betterment.

With respect to individuals JBS's principles were quite simple: help the helpless, as did the Good Samaritan, especially the victims of tragedy; give financial assistance to further the education of able and hard-working youths; reward those who have proved themselves worthy. The giver should give without fanfare and without the expectation of return. Generosity has its own reward.

Such was the dynamic and abiding faith of John Ben Snow, a good man, who departed this life after a short illness on January 21, 1973. Three days later several hundred Americans from many parts of the nation gathered in Colorado Springs to pay their respects and eulogize JBS. He was subsequently buried, after a short graveside ceremony, in the Snow family plot in Pulaski.

IX

The Legacy

John Ben Snow's spirit lives on in a variety of ways. He is still remembered by long-time residents in Pulaski and to their children has become a local legend. His life is the subject of numerous essays and speeches in the local schools. His biography has become required reading in some English classes. Many artifacts and photographs on continuous display outside the public library provide visual reminders of his colorful life in England and Colorado. Plaques and monuments testify to his generosity. But, more important, John Ben Snow left his imprint on six organizations—three business enterprises and three charities.

Woolworth Ltd. remains one of England's foremost retail giants. While its personnel are now all British and their merchandising methods have changed since instituted in the early decades of this century, the sales remain large with the profitability sometimes exceeding the American branch of Woolworth International. Many of those stores opened by Surefire Snow are still operating profitably, several in the same locations. Some will doubtless celebrate their centennial in the original locations.

The Western Horseman continues to thrive as a magazine and a business corporation. JBS's shares were sold shortly after his death to the management team he had put in place. Dick Spencer, who had become publisher on Don Flint's retirement in 1969, became chairman of the board and served in both capacities until his death in July 1989. The format has changed little since Snow's death, although the advertising has increased. According to Randy Witte, the present publisher, the circulation has steadily increased to 200,000 paid subscribers and newsstand buyers. The firm employs twenty-nine persons today and occupies the same building in Colorado Springs. That *The Western Horseman* remains the premier magazine among horse lovers is a tribute to JBS and the personnel he selected to succeed him.

In contrast, Speidel Newspapers, Inc., no longer exists as a corporate entity, though many of the onetime executives and employees occasionally gather to exchange memories and toast their founder and benefactor. Most of the executives became millionaires, thanks to the profit-sharing plans instituted by JBS; some accumulated more wealth than their benefactor. The nonmanagerial employees are secure with adequate pensions.

The demise of Speidel Newspapers occurred much faster than anyone in the organization anticipated or desired. In 1972, one year before Snow's death, Speidel Newspapers went public with a large issue of common stock. Though many blocks of shares were held by Speidel executives, others were quickly bought up by private and institutional investors without any ties or loyalty to SNI. The profit record of the company had been a good one and its future was promising; to many investors it was an attractive investment.

However, once public, Speidel Newspapers also became attractive to rival news chains and press barons interested in expanding their own empires. In fact, it was ripe for a takeover by hostile publishers in both the United States and Canada. Speidel management resorted to several defensive measures to fend off a hostile takeover. They pushed for protective legislation in state legislatures. They sought laws in Washington. They bought back some of their own stock. But these measures were not sufficient to deter a takeover bid from a well-known Canadian press baron.

To forestall this probability, the SNI board of directors decided to seek out a friendly merger with a sister chain of newspapers. The negotiators talked with several family-owned chains; but the most advantageous terms came from the Gannett Newspapers, the Rochester-based firm then under the leadership of Al Neuharth. Within months, after a rapid series of negotiations and decisions completed by Rollan Melton, then chairman of the board, Speidel merged with Gannett to form the nation's largest chain of newspapers. The terms involved an exchange of stock, protection of employee benefits, and some personnel guarantees.

Gannett benefited considerably from this merger. The Speidel papers consistently produced profits above the chain average. Most of the Speidel managers remained with their own papers, although several have since retired. A few of the Speidel board members secured seats on the enlarged Gannett board. While neither Merritt Speidel nor John Ben Snow would have welcomed a merger with any chain, they would have agreed that the Gannett merger was the least of several evils. It is interesting to note that in the 1930s Merritt Speidel had lauded the Gannett family chain and suggested it to JBS as a model well worth emulating.

JBS also left his imprint on the charitable foundation which bears his name. When it was established in 1948, he selected the original members and presided at the annual meetings. The earliest meetings were usually held in New York City at the Irving Trust Company or the New York Athletic Club. After 1960 they took place in Colorado Springs at JBS's office in the Mining Exchange Building. Most meetings were short, informal, and followed by food and drinks at the El Paso Club. All of the official transactions were recorded in the corporate minute book by Talbot Malcolm, secretary and treasurer for several decades.

In 1969 John Ben Snow enlarged the membership of the Snow Foundation from five to seven in order to include two associates from Speidel Newspapers. Since his death in 1973 the membership has been drawn from three constituencies: (1) the Snow family, (2) the Malcolm family, and (3) the ex-Speidel executives. The Foundation still meets annually, usually in mid-June, and its seven members come from various parts of the United States and diverse occupational backgrounds.

The corpus of the Snow Foundation was formed through the annual contributions of JBS between 1949 and 1972. These early gifts, charted in Table I (*see p. 150*), varied from $10,000 in 1953 to $1,000,000 in 1966, although the latter was in fact passed through the Foundation as a grant to the Newhouse School of Syracuse University to establish a research chair in journalism. His average annual gift to the Foundation amounted to $62,500. The accumulated value of these gifts was slightly more than $1,500,000 in 1972. The market value of the corpus varied from year to year, as Table I also reveals. It did not appreciate much in value because the size and number of annual grants increased at a faster rate than the corpus, so that in some years the grants exceeded the income.

This growth profile reflected the philosophy and policies of the original members. Their goals were threefold: (1) preservation of the capital, (2) maximization of income, and (3) liberal distribution of income through grants. During his life JBS made all of the investment decisions related to the foundation. However, shortly after his death the members agreed to secure the financial services of a portfolio manager at the Irving Trust Company. The current provider of those services is The Bank of New York.

Since JBS's death the Snow Foundation has become more proactive and professional in its grant-making policies and procedures. The annual meetings have become more formal with an agenda, reports, and full discussions. The increased work load has led to a division of labor, standing committees, and compensation for those members who serve as staff. A trustee-managed foundation with only part-time secretarial help, there is no bureaucracy, and all members are accessible to grantees. All inquiries and proposals received are posted on a computer located in Pulaski, the official center, screened by a grant committee, and voted upon individually at the annual meeting. Interviews and site visits are conducted by the board members. A post-grant evaluation system will soon be in place.

Since 1972 the assets of the Snow Foundation have more than tripled, from $1,500,000 to slightly over $5,000,000 in 1992. The income, expenses, and grants have increased overall, but at different rates, as Table II (*see p. 151*) demonstrates. Whereas before 1972 the members often approved grants totaling more than the income, since then they have adhered closely to the 5 percent mandated by the Tax Reform Act of 1969. The financial managers, moreover, have opted for a more diversified portfolio to insure steady appreciation of assets and income. The rate of the expenses, which increased considerably shortly after the founder's death, has leveled off in recent years, while the size and number of grants have followed a similar pattern.

Most of the funds distributed by the Snow Foundation have benefited individuals and organizations located in central New York. Within this rather broad spectrum there are clear patterns and trends that deserve comment. A large number of grants reflect JBS's desire to improve the quality of life in Pulaski and its environs. The numerous scholarship grants reflect his preference for investing in human beings, especially needy persons with talents, rather than in bricks and mortar. Numerous grants have been made to youth-oriented organizations, while others have assisted the local Baptist Church and Society. Most reflect the donor's interests, preferences, and values. There is no way of knowing how many lives his generosity has influenced.

To demonstrate his love and feelings of kinship, John Ben Snow also established the Snow Family Trust by setting aside an endowment fund of $1,000,000 in his estate and specifying that the annual income should be distributed to persons related to him by blood or marriage. The first trustees were Ralph W. Snow of Pulaski, New York, the family representative; Talbot Malcolm of Westfield, New Jersey, the testator's attorney; and Henry McKenzie of New York City, the corporate trustee from the Irving Trust Company. These original trustees were gradually succeeded by the present author; Allen R. Malcolm, a retired attorney from Westfield, New Jersey; and Donna Daniels, who represents The Bank of New York.

The current trustees meet annually in mid-December in New York City to assess the portfolio of the endowment and allot the annual income to qualified distributees. The present author administers the day-to-day activities from the office in Pulaski. The official family tree, which has been computerized, serves as the basis for all distributions. Since 1973 over three hundred members of the Snow family have received over $700,000 from the endowment. A system of rotation insures equity and fairness. Presently the family tree contains over six hundred descendents of Benjamin Snow, Sr., who settled in Pulaski in 1821, and the number of qualified descendants increases each year because of longevity and the inclusion of twenty-one-year olds. By the middle of the next century, when the Snow Family Trust will terminate, untold hundreds of Snows will have benefited from the largesse of John Ben Snow.

The largest of the philanthropic organizations established by JBS is the Snow Memorial Trust, a memorial to his parents formed from the residual assets in his estate. The original trustees were Ralph Snow, Talbot Malcolm, Henry McKenzie, and Charles Stout of Reno, Nevada. They have since been succeeded by the present author, Allen Malcolm, and Rollan Melton, head of Gannett West in Reno. Joseph Mitchell of Reid and Priest, New York City, serves as legal counsel, while Donna Daniels represents The Bank of New York. The official address remains Box 378, Pulaski, New York.

The purposes of this Trust, as stated in the will, were to distribute funds "to organizations operated exclusively for religious, charitable, scientific, literary, or educational purposes, or for the prevention of cruelty to children or animals." Because the first trustees considered these purposes too general, they decided to focus on three geographical areas: central New York, in accordance with the donor's mandate; metropolitan New York, where JBS went to school and lived for several years; and Reno, Nevada, the onetime headquarters of Speidel Newspapers. While a few grants have been made elsewhere, most of the funds have gone to projects within these areas.

The assets of the Snow Memorial Trust have increased from $11,000,000 in 1976 to nearly $20,000,000 in 1992. (*See Table III, p. 152*) This growth reflects the conservative financial philosophy of the trustees and their portfolio managers at the Irving Trust Company and The Bank of New York. Since the primary mission of the charitable trust is to support worthy nonprofit causes into the twenty-first century, preservation of the corpus is paramount. The second principle is the maximization of income, while the third is growth roughly equivalent to the rate of inflation so that the dollar value remains about the same.

The largest single grant of the Snow Memorial Trust, over $1,200,000, was made to the village of Pulaski in 1975 to construct a memorial to JBS's parents. This project had, in fact, been mandated by the testator, although the details were left to a citizens' committee working with Ralph Snow and the present author. The edifice, located in the heart of the village on Jefferson Street, houses the public library, village offices, the police department, a board room for the trustees of the village, a meeting hall, and an office for the Snow philanthropies. The building was opened and dedicated on 16 June 1976 during the annual meeting of the Snow Foundation.

To insure that the memorial edifice was properly maintained, JBS also established an endowment within the Snow Family Trust. The Family Trustee was made responsible for overseeing the maintenance of the building and administering the funds. Thanks to the generosity and foresight of John Ben Snow, hundreds of Pulaskians and thousands of central New Yorkers use and enjoy the library, the offices, and the meeting rooms of the Snow Memorial.

In 1976 the trustees committed over $1,000,000 in seed money to initiate the publication of *The Dial*. This monthly program guide, started under the aegis of Channel 13 in New York City and its head, Jay Iselin, was a unique experiment in multimedia journalism. Though undercapitalized from its inception, *The Dial* provided intelligent comment and criticism to a national audience for over six years. It also brought some unity to the diverse world of public television. But because of high production costs and limited advertising income, the magazine ceased publication in 1983, and the program-related investment (PRI) was converted to a grant.

Since its inception the Snow Memorial Trust has granted several million dollars to the professional education of lawyers, engineers, businessmen, librarians, and curators. Actually John Ben Snow began underwriting legal scholarships at New York University Law School in 1958 and continued to do so until his death. Since 1976 the Snow Scholarships have been funded by the Memorial Trust, and the recipients have been an intergral part of the Root-Tilden Program, which emphasizes public service. Among the alumni of this program are numerous public servants, state and federal judges, and politicians, including one United States Senator and a cabinet officer.

For more than a decade the trustees have also funded undergraduate scholarships at the NYU School of Business and Public Administration and at the Newhouse School of Communications at Syracuse University. At Clarkson University in Potsdam, New York, several Native American students from the nearby reservation have benefited each year from trust funds. The training program for museum curators at Cooperstown and Oneonta has received several grants, while a three-year internship program in library science at Syracuse University was started with seed money from the Trust. Thus the financial assistance rendered by the Trust has enabled hundreds of young women and men to complete their education and launch their professional careers. Most of the recipients have come from nonaffluent families; many have been women and minorities.

The trustees have chosen to commit substantial moneys to midcareer professional education. The National Judicial College in Reno, Nevada, the recipient of several grants, provides state and local judges, especially newly elected and appointed judges, with classes and seminars in both the procedural and substantive aspects of the law. The American Press Institute of Reston, Virginia, which has received many grants, gives journalists and editors training workshops to improve their performance and keep them informed of ever-changing technology. Cambridge College in Cambridge, Massachusetts, provides midcareer professionals with the opportunity to make a career switch, especially to education and human services. The selecton of the participants in each of these programs is made by the grantee rather than the trustees, although the names of the beneficiaries are included in the progress reports.

From these and other grants countless individuals and nonprofit organizations have benefited as a result of the largesse of John Ben Snow. The files and archives in Pulaski are filled with testimonials expressing gratitude to the donor or his trustees. The progress and final reports testify to the benefits of a program or the impact of a grant. The ongoing evaluation of all programs, a process launched in 1991, will serve as the basis for a history of the Snow Foundation and Trust.

It is impossible, finally, to enumerate the countless beneficiaries of JBS's philanthropy, but it is clear that thousands of Americans have enjoyed the fruits of his generosity. He was a good man with a large heart. May his spirit of generosity live on!

TABLE I

JBS Gifts and Foundation Assets and Income
1949-1972

	GIFTS	ACCUMULATIVE	ASSETS	INCOME
1949	25,070.00	25,070.00	24,488	1,107
1950	24,375.00	49,445.00	50,036	1,377
1951	25,000.00	74,445.00	66,528	1,716
1952	115,000.00	189,445.00	170,064	4,290
1953	10,000.00	199,445.00	163,635	8,680
1954	69,409.06	268,854.06	227,985	11,100
1955	71,200.00	341,054.06	309,561	16,593
1956	77,500.00	418,554.06	855,995	23,643
1957	100,000.00	518,554.06	629,451	149,273
1958	90,000.00	608,554.06	666,557	35,539
1959	107,515.00	716,019.06	781,971	38,464
1960	25,000.00	741,019.06	819,320	44,490
1961	124,600.00	865,619.06	923,712	48,124
1962	77,850.00	943,469.06	1,027,811	48,791
1963	66,025.00	1,009,494.06	1,093,642	64,066
1964	60,000.00	1,069,494.06	1,146,420	110,095
1965	70,000.00	1,139,494.06	1,136,507	80,140
1966	1,000,000.00*	1,139,494.06	964,829	NA
1967	99,187.50	1,238,681.56	1,095,873	65,379
1968	100,000.00	1,338,681.56	1,226,865	67,050
1969	100,000.00	1,438,681.56	1,374,123	76,081
1970	57,000.00	1,495,681.56	1,439,015	84,457
1971	105,000.00	1,500,681.56	1,486,409	126,340
1972	—0—	1,500,681.56	1,467,965	82,600

* In this year the donor contributed $1,000,000 as a pass-through grant to Syracuse University.

TABLE II

John Ben Snow Foundation Assets and Grants

	ASSETS	INCOME	EXPENSES	GRANTS
1973	1,486,151	91,750	15,783	59,300
1974	1,867,230	505,545	19,565	101,800
1975	1,846,275	128,281	16,042	107,840
1976	1,974,489	959,824	13,261	805,677
1977	2,224,777	723,903	15,537	442,365
1978	2,456,691	451,092	18,690	216,000
1979	3,859,574	347,248	29,669	265,685
1980	3,956,733	382,368	33,206	736,892
1981	4,570,682	650,309	57,470	580,350
1982	4,729,272	534,617	81,459	198,700
1983	5,131,428	667,452	93,276	163,250
1984	3,175,920	257,096	78,042	161,300
1985	3,321,361	301,536	84,754	132,700
1986	3,354,686	492,176	79,205	189,400
1987	4,451,964	539,287	97,298	152,800
1988	3,835,196	326,703	94,522	152,800
1989	4,015,631	428,277	91,015	162,095
1990	4,093,523	362,382	93,161	192,350
1991	4,185,440	389,265	94,151	184,575

TABLE III

Memorial Trust Grants by the Year

	ASSETS	GROSS INCOME	GRANT TOTAL
1976	11,037,712	722,750	716,330
1977	10,984,800	786,033	482,249
1978	13,049,325	937,215	509,446
1979	13,501,732	1,074,853	2,180,984
1980	12,545,047	1,078,725	810,000
1981	11,767,343	1,050,336	1,778,500
1982	12,447,463	1,003,666	716,735
1983	13,247,005	1,088,015	916,464
1984	14,049,116	1,200,386	1,060,938
1985	15,978,381	1,229,668	1,160,289
1986	17,135,477	1,267,223	1,124,000
1987	16,279,023	1,275,298	961,380
1988	16,940,555	1,253,903	836,840
1989	18,964,617	1,529,494	1,070,300
1990	18,563,279	1,300,433	957,300